SENSATIONAL

SALADS

SENSATIONAL

SALADS

LIONEL MARTINEZ

GALLERY BOOKS
An imprint of W. H. Smith Publishers Inc.
112 Madison Avenue
New York, New York 10016

A QUARTO BOOK

Published by Gallery Books
an imprint of W. H. Smith Publishers Inc.
112 Madison Avenue, New York, N.Y. 10016

ISBN 0-8317-7665-X

Typeset in London by QV Typesetting Ltd., London
Color origination by Hong Kong Scanner Craft Ltd.
Printed by Lee Fung Asco Printers Ltd.

This Book was designed and produced by
Footnote Productions Ltd/Quarto Publishing Ltd.
6 Blundell Street, London N7 9BH

Home Economist Stella Murphy
Photography by Clive Boden

Designer Hazel Edington
Art Editor Nick Clark
Art Director Alastair Campbell
Editors Nicoletta Flessati, Sally Wood
Managing Editor Jim Miles
Editorial Director Sheila Rosenzweig
Paste Up Leaper and Gard Ltd., Bristol

Contents

ESSEN

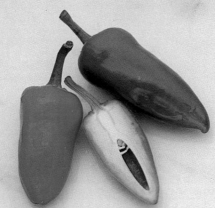

This section
the basic raw
combine succ
salad and shows how
salads using garnishes.

TIALS

takes a detailed look at

ingredients that will

essfully to make up a

to add glamor to your

Salad Greens

The word salad derives from the Latin word *sal*, which means salt. The Romans used salt to dress their green salads as well as using it as a food preservative; hence the extension to 'salad'.

Larousse defines salads as 'Dishes made up of herbs, plants, vegetables, eggs, meat and fish, seasoned with oil, vinegar, salt and pepper, with or without other ingredients.' In Europe until the late eighteenth century, salads were the provender of nobility. It took the French Revolution to free the chefs from the strains of noble employment and allow them to seek a new way to make a living. This heralded the birth of the classic French restaurant which introduced salads to the general public.

Today, salads have an international flavor. Indian, Mexican, Thai and South American cuisines are but a few of those that have found their way to our tables. Japanese salads are a visual bouquet with ingredients cut into fans, curly shavings, rectangles and blossoms, all beautifully arranged on the serving plate. African salads use ingredients such as plantains, yams, breadfruit and cassava as well as more familiar greens. South American and Thai salads tend to use spicy dressings. Chinese salads call for well-seasoned dressings and sometimes include such strange fare as dried jellyfish. In short, there is a world full of salads for every palate.

THE GREEN SALAD

When should you serve the green or mixed green salad? History gives us a few hints. During the reign of Domitian at the height of the Roman Empire, during the first century AD, green salads progressed from being served last to being served first. The reason for this change is not clear. It is known that some Romans thought that green salads served last induced sleep. In Renaissance Italy, banquets began with lavish and complicated salads. Louis XIV of France was also a salad king. He consumed vast amounts of salad at the beginning, middle and end of every meal. Another famous salad-fancier, on a smaller scale, was French author Alexandre Dumas. He preferred his salad last. Today, salads are sometimes served last as an aid to the digestion of a rich meal; first, when the meal is simple but the salad is complex; alone when people are watching their waistlines. When should you serve your green salad? It's entirely up to you.

PREPARING SALAD GREENS

Freshness is the key when buying greens. Wilted greens are greens that have lost a good deal of their water content. In today's world of modern refrigeration and transportation there is no excuse for wilted greens at the market. Once you arrive home with your fresh salad greens, they should be washed immediately. Washing all the greens at once makes a lot more sense than washing some each time you make a salad.

To wash any leafy green, including tight-head lettuces and cabbage, carefully separate the leaves and rinse under cold running water. Inspect for dirt near the center and at the bottom of each leaf. Always discard any wilted or bruised leaves.

When making a salad it is important to have dry salad greens. Residual water has two unpleasant effects. One, water left on salad greens will wilt the leaves. Two, water left on the leaves will dilute and change the flavor of even the heartiest dressings. To dry salad greens, either pat the leaves dry with a paper towel or drain them well in a colander or (my preference) spin them in a salad drier.

Before storing the greens you might want to tear them (never cut) into bite-sized pieces. Wrap the greens in either a cloth or paper towel, leaf by leaf if you wish. Put the towel-wrapped greens in a plastic bag and put the bag in the vegetable compartment of your refrigerator. By doing this you will be sure of having crisp greens on the table.

Great variety is possible in salad-making. Green salads can be made with lettuce, green pepper, watercress, spinach, endive, chicory, cucumber and many other green vegetables and are usually tossed in a dressing. The most popular of these are French (oil, vinegar, salt and pepper) and mayonnaise. In mixed salads, other raw vegetables frequently used are: cabbage, carrots, cauliflower, celery, onions, radishes and tomatoes. The fresher the better.

Lettuces

Ingredients for green or mixed salads fall into three categories. The first is lettuce: Boston, iceberg and so on. Vegetables and herbs that double as salad greens are the second group. All the extras, such as pine nuts and bean sprouts, form the third category

Chicory also called curly endive, or endive in Britain. Its bitter flavor has been called sharp and appealing. The leaves at the center have a milder taste than the outer ones. Usually used in combination with other salad greens.

Endive also called Belgian endive, witloof or French endive. Those familiar with endive say it has a delicately bitter flavor. It is the cleanest of all 'lettuce' and a prized member of the misunderstood endive family.

Pak-choi a Chinese green now cultivated in

Europe. It is recognizable by its chalk-white stalks. Both the succulent stalks and the soft leaves have a mild cabbage flavor.

Chinese cabbage also called celery cabbage. The taste has been described as a cross between cabbage and celery. Native to China and eastern Asia, Chinese cabbage really belongs to the mustard family. With the shape of romaine lettuce and the denseness of cabbage, the crisp leaves will take the heaviest of dressings.

Watercress delicate and pungent with a taste that

Endive

Pak-choi

Chicory

Iceberg lettuce

Romaine lettuce

Radicchio

Spinach

Chinese cabbage

Watercress

Oakleaf lettuce

11

Boston lettuce

Webb's lettuce

Lamb's lettuce

Chinese broccoli

Mignonette lettuce

Choy sum

Sorrel

Cress

has also been described as peppery. It is a member of the mustard clan and was known to the Greeks in 4000 BC. Watercress leaves are fragile and bruise easily so care should be taken when washing and storing. Do not store for more than two days.

Oakleaf lettuce an unusual, loose-headed lettuce with a distinctive flavor.

Spinach a versatile vegetable, which can be used in anything from soups to stuffings. As a salad green it brings a deep, rich green to the salad bowl as well as its own unique taste. After decades of being cooked to a slimy mush, or known only as Popeye's stuff, spinach has become a respected vegetable and salad green again. Spinach will bruise easily so be careful when washing and tearing the leaves.

Radicchio an Italian endive. It comes in two colorful varieties: rosso, which has pink to dark red leaves with white veins, and castelfranco, which has green leaves with multicolored flecks. Radicchio's flavor has been called distinctive.

Iceberg lettuce also called crisphead and head lettuce. The hearts of iceberg lettuce have an interesting flavor, the leaves have almost none. Iceberg lettuce is very crisp and will take the heaviest of salad dressings without wilting... and without any loss in iceberg taste. This is the most widely sold lettuce in the U.S.A.

Romaine lettuce also called cos. This lettuce has been characterized as having a strong, sharp, appealingly pungent taste. A very popular lettuce, it is flavorful either by itself or in combination with other greens.

Mignonette lettuce similar to a romaine lettuce in form, this lettuce has dark-green or red-tinged outer leaves and a good flavor.

Choy sum also called Chinese flowering cabbage. Recognizable by its small yellow flowers and grooved stems, a green with a mild cabbage flavor. The leaves are used whole or chopped.

Chinese broccoli also known as Chinese kale. With a more pronounced cabbage flavor than choy sum, the stalks of this green are particularly delicious. Prepare and use as you would ordinary broccoli (the flowering top of a cabbage).

Sorrel Also called dock and sourgrass. Its flavor is lemony, sour and tart. Sorrel is grown commercially and is also found in the wild. Sorrel grown in France is the mildest in acidity. For salads it is best to use the tender young leaves.

Cress a grouping which encompasses garden cress, upland cress and winter cress. Their taste is mildly sharp. They all make good garnishes for mixed green salads.

Webb's lettuce a lettuce variety that is widely cultivated. It has curly leaves and is crisper than the soft-leaved Boston lettuce.

Boston lettuce also called butterhead or cabbage lettuce. A subtle, sweet, buttery flavor distinguishes this salad green. It is an excellent component in any salad and takes dressings well. Care must be taken when washing it as it is fragile.

Lamb's lettuce also called corn salad, mâche, field salad and lamb's tongue. It has a tangy taste. Both wild and cultivated in Europe, it does not travel well so it is usually only available at local markets near where it is grown or picked.

A Bunch of Herbs

A good working knowledge of the taste of different herbs is very helpful when it comes to making salad dressings. It's fairly easy to describe the flavor of a single herb just by comparing it to something else.

Fresh herbs add color as well as flavor to salads and salad dressings. Unless sprigs of fresh herbs are being used as a garnish, they should be very finely chopped. Dried herbs must be handled differently. The substitution ratio is between one-third to one-half dried herbs to fresh. If a recipe calls for one tablespoon of fresh basil, for example, substitute about one teaspoon of dried basil. However, before adding the dried herb to your recipe, either: add the dried herbs to 1 to 2 tablespoons of any liquid called for in the recipe. Let stand for at least 25 minutes, then use, or: crush the dried herbs between your fingers until they are powdered and then add them to the salad. The first method will release more herb flavor than the second.

Fresh herbs can be stored in either of two ways: 1. Wash and completely dry the fresh herbs. Place them in a jar and tightly seal it. Put the jar in the refrigerator until ready to use. 2. Wrap the herbs in a damp paper towel and refrigerate until ready to use. Store fresh herbs whole. Do any cutting or chopping necessary when you are ready to use them.

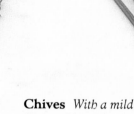

Sage *A pungent, perennial herb that can be over-powering so should be used sparingly. Often used in stuffings, sage enhances veal, pork and duck.*

Dill *The taste of this fragrant herb is slightly reminiscent of caraway seeds. It is frequently used in cucumber, fish and egg salads.*

Chives *With a mild onion flavor, chives are easy to grow. Good in dressings and salads.*

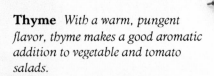

Balm *When using this lemon-scented herb in fruit and vegetable salads, decrease the amount of vinegar or lemon juice in the dressing.*

Mint *Mint has a refreshing taste that cannot be compared to anything else. Use in yogurt dressings, vegetable salads and tabouleh.*

Thyme *With a warm, pungent flavor, thyme makes a good aromatic addition to vegetable and tomato salads.*

Coriander *Also known as cilantro and Chinese parsley, coriander's distinctive flavor is found in Asian and Caribbean salads.*

Basil *This pungent member of the mint family is reminiscent of cloves with a hint of licorice. Use it on vegetable and green salads.*

Rosemary *An evergreen aromatic herb, rosemary should be used sparingly; its clean, woody taste is ideal for poultry and meat salads.*

Parsley *A universal herb with a strong, agreeable flavor. It goes well with any salad except fruit.*

Marjoram *Marjoram has a sweet spicy taste and is a good addition to mixed green, zucchini and chicken salads.*

Fennel *This anise-flavored herb comes in seed and leaf form. It can be used as a substitute for celery and parsley in salads.*

Bay leaf *This bitter, spicy and pungent leaf comes from an evergreen tree. It works well in cold rice and pasta salads and in tomato dressings.*

Lemon geranium *Mainly used as a garnish and for its decorative leaves which impart a lemony fragrance. Can be used with fish salads.*

Dried Herbs and Spices

The potency of dried herbs and spices comes from their flavorful oils and esters. These will evaporate over time; the process is accelerated by incorrect storage, so be sure to keep them dry.

While it is always preferable to use fresh herbs, most spices are by definition dried. For example, peppercorns are dried berries, cloves are the dried bud of the clove tree, cinnamon is ground from dried bark, nutmeg is a dried kernel, and turmeric is a dried root. Even so, freshness is still important.

Many health-food shops sell herbs and spices loose in their whole form. Not only is this a much better way to buy your ingredients, it is usually much cheaper as well. Do not store dried herbs and spices near the stove or any other warm place. Heat will cause them to lose their strength fast. They should be kept in a dry, cool, dark place.

Put hot chili peppers in a brown paper bag before you store them in the refrigerator. This keeps the oils in the chilies from evaporating. To store ginger root, either keep it at room temperature or bury the root in moist earth or sand. It will keep for months.

Red chili pepper flakes/ ground chili *When red chili peppers are dried and ground the resulting powder is extremely hot and spicy. Flakes are often used in salads and dressings too.*

Cumin *Belonging to the carrot family, ground cumin is an important carminative element in curry and chili powders. The dried whole seeds are also used for flavoring.*

Poppy seeds *The seeds of the poppy plant are used extensively in Eastern European, Middle Eastern and Indian cookery. They have a pleasanily nutty taste and texture.*

Celery seeds *The dried seeds of the familiar celery plant. They are used in soups, egg dishes and in certain salads.*

Cinnamon *The dried, ground bark of the cinnamon tree (a member of the laurel family). Light yellowish-brown in color, its tangy aromatic flavor goes well with fruit salads.*

Dried chervil *Related to sweet parsley with a peppery after-taste, this herb has been touted as 'gourmet's parsley'. It enhances green, tomato, potato and egg salads.*

Dill weed *Related to the parsley family, fresh dill is a feathery herb. When chopped and dried it is called dill weed and has a taste that is reminiscent of caraway.*

Ginger *The root of a perennial plant, ginger is best used fresh. Dried ground ginger is the flavoring element in many cakes and biscuits and may be added to fruit salads.*

   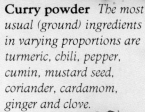

Dried oregano *Related to marjoram, oregano was popularized as the 'pizza herb'. It has a strong and aromatic taste and may be used to add zest to most types of seafood.*

Cardamom pods *Obtained from a perennial plant related to ginger, the seeds are ground for use as an aromatic ingredient in spice mixtures like curry powder.*

Mace *This is the fibrous outer covering of the nutmeg. Use ground mace in fruit salads, chocolate puddings and cakes to bring out a mild nutmeg flavor.*

Curry powder *The most usual (ground) ingredients in varying proportions are turmeric, chili, pepper, cumin, mustard seed, coriander, cardamom, ginger and clove.*

Thyme *Thyme has a strong, sharp taste. The leaves, from a perennial plant of the mint family, can be used fresh or dried and form the basis of bouquet garnis.*

Cayenne pepper *A very hot red pepper made from dried and ground red chili peppers. Should always be used sparingly. Suitable for cheese and fish dishes, curries and marinades.*

White peppercorns *Pepper berries grow on perennial vines. White peppercorns are left on the vines until completely ripe, when the outer hulls split and are removed.*

Black peppercorns *More pungent than white peppercorns, these are picked from the vines before fully ripe. When ground, they produce both black and white particles.*

 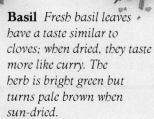 

Marjoram *Aromatic with minty overtones, this grey-green herb consists of the dried leaves of a perennial herb belonging to the mint family. Can be used fresh or dried.*

Dried tarragon *With its slightly anise taste, tarragon is a popular herb for egg, chicken, mixed green and seafood salads, as well as in salad dressings and French vinegars.*

Basil *Fresh basil leaves have a taste similar to cloves; when dried, they taste more like curry. The herb is bright green but turns pale brown when sun-dried.*

Mint *Only spearmint and peppermint have culinary applications. Mint has a strong, sweet, tangy and distinctive flavor. The leaves can be used fresh or dried.*

Extra Ingredients

From the basic primary foods available worldwide, different races have, over the centuries, developed many variations in taste and texture. As new flavors and combinations are always being discovered, there need never be a jaded palate.

Until quite recently, salads tended to consist of a tasteless concoction of lettuce, tomato and cucumber and were served only on hot summer days. Now, because they spell 'health', salads are at the peak of their popularity. They are many and varied and can include more or less any ingredient. All that is required is a little imagination and willingness to experiment. The most popular salads (such as *Salade Niçoise* from France (with lettuce, tuna, olives, and hard-cooked eggs); Greek Salad (with feta cheese, tomatoes, onions and olives); and Waldorf Salad (with apples, celery, walnuts and dates), always have a pleasing balance of color, flavor and texture so that they appeal both to the eye and to the palate.

Here are some less obvious ingredients that can be used successfully in salads. Nuts, for instance, are an often-neglected food. Dating to pre-agricultural times as a source of both food and oil, they are versatile enough to be used in many types of salad.

Almonds *After they have been shelled, almonds are blanched to remove the bitter skins. They may be used whole, flaked or chopped.*

Bean sprouts *These are beans (usually soya) that have germinated producing crunchy nutritious shoots about 2 in (5 cm) long.*

Lotus root (left) *Crunchy and bland, prized for the decorative pattern of the sliced root.* **Bamboo shoots** *Crisp texture and mild taste.*

Mung bean sprouts *The sprouted shoots of the tiny green mung bean are frequently used in oriental or health-food salads.*

Brown lentils *Small whole lentils — other varieties are red, orange or green and either whole or split. Lentils cook quickly and add bulk to salads.*

Cashews *Crunchy, flavorsome nuts that are usually sold shelled. Avoid using ready-salted cashews as salad ingredients.*

Cannellini beans *Italian white beans similar to haricot beans. They add substance as well as flavor to a salad and take dressings well.*

Tofu (Bean curd) *Sold in cakes, fresh bean curd has a delicate texture and clean fragrance. Bean curd is made from yellow soya beans.*

Cracked wheat (burghul) *The wheat grains are cooked and cracked to make them digestible so that only a brief soaking is required before eating.*

Water chestnuts *Available fresh or peeled in cans, the crisp white flesh of the water chestnut is added to many Chinese dishes and salads.*

Walnuts *Distinctive looking and strong-tasting, halved or chopped walnuts have long been a popular addition to the salad bowl.*

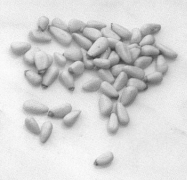

Pine nuts *These nuts have a sweet flavor and contain a lot of oil. They are used extensively in the cuisines of Italy, Greece and the Middle East.*

Couscous *A grain product derived from durum wheat. The bland flavor is enlivened in salads by the addition of herbs and spices.*

Chick peas *These mealy, substantial pulses have a sweetly bland flavor that blends well. Available dried and uncooked or cooked in cans.*

Capers *Flower buds from a mustard plant, capers are usually pickled and have a sour, salty taste. They are good additions to potato and meat salads.*

Equipment

A well-equipped kitchen can make all the difference to the quality of your cooking — and can transform the preparation of meals from a chore to a positive pleasure.

Perhaps the most important factor of all is your collection of kitchen utensils.

A series of sharp kitchen knives in particular will bring you pure joy: invest at the very least in a large all-purpose cook's knife that will cut or chop virtually anything; a smaller one for coring and slicing and a serrated-edge one for paring, peeling and slicing soft vegetables and fruit. The best knives have blades riveted into the handle. Accurate measuring spoons are useful, as are wooden spoons for stirring and mixing — the more the merrier. A sturdy chopping board is invaluable, as are: a pair of kitchen scissors for cutting the rind off bacon and snipping herbs; a pestle and mortar for crushing herbs and spices, or blending them with other ingredients; and pepper and salt mills containing whole peppercorns and coarse salt granules so that you will always have fresh seasonings.

It is also worth investing in a salad shaker to shake the excess water from washed salad greens; a double-bladed herb chopper for finely chopping herbs and other salad ingredients without bruising delicate leaves; a wire whisk for stirring and whisking sauces and dressings; a vegetable peeler with a swivel blade for thinly peeling vegetables; a garlic crusher for mincing garlic and extracting the juice from the garlic cloves; and a grater with several different grating surfaces and a slicing blade.

1
2
3
4
5
6
7

1 *Salad shaker.*
2 *Kitchen knives.*
3 *Double-bladed herb chopper.*
4 *Cleaver. For jointing meat and poultry.*
5 *Grapefruit knife. With a curved tip, for scooping out grapefruit flesh.*
6 *Wooden spoon.*
7 *Wire whisk.*
8 *Mandolin.*
9 *Kitchen scissors.*
10 *Chopping board.*
11 *Egg-slicer.*
12 *Garlic crusher.*
13 *Pestle and mortar.*
14 *Vegetable peeler.*
15 *Grater.*
16 *Pepper and salt mills.*

Garnishes

A garnish is a decorative trimming added to a dish for the table. The word garnish is applied to savory food; decoration more usually refers to sweet food.

As a basic rule of thumb, the garnish or decoration should always have some connection with the ingredients used in the dish to be garnished; for example, whole turned mushrooms would go well with a mushroom quiche. In this way, garnishes can also indicate the ingredients that constitute the dish.

Try to keep the main dish and the garnish at about the same temperature — a cold vegetable garnish on hot food may not be very appetizing.

Since garnishes are largely decorative, the choice of plate on which to display the food is important if you want to achieve a real visual treat. A variety of different shaped plates with light patterns look more attractive than a series of plain, similar shaped plates.

Having chosen your garnish and arranged the food on the appropriate plate, bear in mind the following: if the recipe is served with a sauce (or syrup), it is a good idea to coat the food first and only allow the sauce to flow over the plate if you intend covering the whole plate; a partly covered plate looks messy. Keep herb or vegetable garnishes or fruit decorations clean and fresh looking by having them ready to place on the food at the last moment rather than letting them sink into the sauce.

Make sure you have sharp knives for cutting. A canelle knife is useful for cutting strips from cucumbers, for example. Try to keep cut garnishes to a similar size and be sure to use blemish-free and fresh fruit or vegetables.

Cucumber sliced with a canelle knife looks very attractive and requires very little effort. If sliced thinly enough, cones can be formed from the slices.

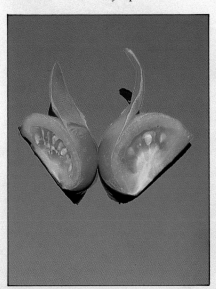

Celery Curls

Top and tail celery and cut into even lengths. Cut down one end of each stick several times but without meeting at the center so the celery remains joined. Either serve like this, or cut the celery curls in half and stand them upright. Place in iced water until they open out.

Orange and Lemon Bows

Cut thin round slices from the fruit. Cut each ring in half. Keeping the slice of lemon or orange joined in the middle, cut through the outer edge and open out to form a bow.

Radish Roses

Remove stalk. Cut a row of petal shapes round the radish, keeping them joined at the base. Cut further rows of petal shapes until the top of the radish is reached. Place the radish rose in iced water for several hours until it opens out.

Tomato Butterflies

Cut a firm tomato evenly into quarters keeping it joined at the base. Carefully separate the skin from the flesh, still keeping the tomato joined at one end. Curl back top ends and arrange it in the form of a butterfly.

Orange and Lemon Twists

Thinly slice the fruit into rings. Cut from outer edge to center of each slice and twist.

Radish Fans

Remove base from radish. Slice upwards from base several times. Place in iced water to open out.

Cucumber Rings
Keep skin on cucumber. Slice into rings. Remove seeded part from the center of each slice. Cut through each ring once and join by overlapping to give a chain effect.

Tomato Roses
Take a firm tomato and remove the skin in a continuous strip about 1 cm (½ in) wide. With the flesh side outside, start curling the strip of skin from the base end, forming a bud shape between the fingers.

Gherkin Fans
With a sharp knife, make several incisions lengthwise into the gherkin, keeping it joined at the base. Gently pull out the slices to form a fan. Keep covered.

Radish Lilies
Remove the stalk and, using a small sharp knife, cut through 4 to 6 times, keeping it joined at the base. Place in iced water for several hours until it opens out.

Carrot Rolls
With a potato peeler remove strips from a large, clean carrot. Roll each strip to make a curl and secure with a cocktail stick to keep the shape. Place in iced water for about an hour; remove cocktail stick.

Orange Curls
Thinly slice orange into rings. Cut these in half. Slice the peel from each half segment, stopping 1 cm (½ in) from end. Form a curl with the loose peel.

Use slices of radish slotted into each other to brighten up a salad.

Pepper Tassels
Leave stalk on pepper. Slice the skin lengthwise all round the pepper, stopping about 1 cm (½ in) from the stalk end. Place in iced water until it opens out to form a bell shape.

Tomato Water-Lily
Hold the tomato between thumb and forefingers at the top and bottom and make even zig-zag cuts around the middle with a sharp knife. Carefully separate the two halves.

Green Onion Tassels
Remove the roots from the green onions and trim to about 7.3 cm (3 in). Cut each one lengthwise through the stalk several times to within 4 cm (1½ in) of the end. Place in iced water for about one hour until they open out.

Cucumber Cones
Thinly slice the cucumber into rings. Cut each slice from center to edge. Hold each side and twist to form a cone.

DRES

No salad is

dressing. This

many types

ingredients that may be

combinations and offers

for salad dressings.

SINGS

complete without a tasty

section identifies the

of oil, vinegar and other

used in many different

a wide range of recipes

Oils and Vinegars

If clothes make the man or woman then dressings make the salad. The purpose is the same: to flatter without distracting. As with clothes, the finest available ingredients should be used to dress each salad.

There are four primary bases for salad: oil with vinegar or lemon juice; mayonnaise; Asian soy or fish sauce; and boiled dressings. These basic combinations have given rise to an infinite variety of dressings.

OLIVE OILS

Most salad dressings use oil; the most frequently used oil is olive. To some it is the only oil of any culinary importance. Although this may be an exaggeration, olive oil is one of the oldest oils used in cooking. Its history stretches back 3,000 years to Mesopotamia, the cradle of civilization. No other oil has remained so popular in Western cooking.

Olive oil comes in four quality ratings, based on the processing of the oil and not on the excellence of the olive.

Extra virgin olive oil is the most intensely flavored. It is the product of the first cold pressing of the olive crop. The color of this oil tends to be yellowish-green to dark green, depending on the amount of filtering it has undergone. This is the best olive oil for salads.

Virgin olive oil is deep yellow and is a combination of oil from the last part of the first pressing plus the entire second cold pressing of the olives. It is a moderately flavorful oil, lighter than the extra virgin oils. This oil also makes excellent salad dressings.

Pure olive oil is a commercial grade oil, retaining some olive flavor. It is satisfactory and relatively inexpensive as a salad oil. Pure olive oil is refined, meaning that it is produced from the heat- and solvent-treated olive mash left over from the first two pressings.

Fine olive oil is not to be used for salads. It is manufactured by further refining of the remaining pulp used to produce pure olive oil and may contain other oils or water. Fine olive oil is good for frying, however.

Extra extra virgin olive oil Very dark green to black-green, it is generally too heavy for salads. This expensive, rare oil is produced from the first few twists of the olive press.

The price of olive oil has much to do with which pressing you purchase. Extra virgin olive is about twice as costly as pure olive oil. The country of origin also figures in the pricing of olive oil. French oils, with their light golden color and fruity taste, are the most expensive and are considered by many to be the best in the world. The Greek and Italian olive oils are less costly than the French and are hardy, robust and aromatic. Spanish olive oil is heavy and better used for cooking.

OTHER OILS

Of course, olive oil is not the only oil to be used on salads. The ancient Egyptians made oil from flax and radish seeds. The early Asians utilized soya beans and coconuts as sources for their oil. All these oils are still in use today. One oil definitely not in use today was extracted from the opium poppy by the ancient Greeks. This poppy seed oil must have produced a rather dreamy dressing.

Hazelnut and almond oils These are delicately flavored, nutty oils. They are very light and should be used on delicate salad greens. Not cheap, these oils should be refrigerated to protect their fresh flavor.

Peanut oil Also called groundnut oil, and extensively used in South-East Asian cooking. The peanut flavor is not very pronounced.

Walnut oil A very aromatic oil that imparts a nutty taste to dressings. It also makes an interesting mayonnaise that goes well with chicken salad. Walnut oil is expensive. Keep it under refrigeration to maintain its freshness.

Grape seed oil A rich, full-bodied oil usually found in combination with pepper and/or herbs.

Sesame oil This aromatic oil made from sesame seeds is much used in Asian cooking. It will impart a mysterious savor to subtle dressings.

Sunflower seed, corn, cottonseed, safflower and soya bean oils These rather bland oils give just a hint of their origins in their flavors. Use these oils when a light dressing is desired.

Salad oil This is a mixture of those vegetable oils which, depending on world commodity prices, a manufacturer can buy cheaply. The same brand may contain cottonseed oil mixed with soya oil one month and all corn oil the next. Salad oil is good value if all you want is a bland oil.

VINEGARS

First made by the Chinese over 3,000 years ago, vinegar is the juice of any fruit or grain that has

As well as the quality of the raw
produce involved, a salad's standard
depends on the dressing it is served
with. So make sure the ingredients you
use are the best available (this is
particularly important for the classic
French vinaigrette). Less obvious
ingredients that may be used include
yogurt, soured cream, cheeses, honey,
garlic, herbs and citrus juices.

fermented beyond alcohol and become acidic — acetic acid, to be exact. Its modern name derives from the Gauls, who were introduced to wine when they were conquered by the Romans. The wine was usually spoiled by the time the Romans got around to selling it to the local populace. The Gauls called this potion *vin aigre* or sour wine.

Vinegar should be used in proportion to its strength. This will depend upon the amount of acetic acid that is present. Most vinegars used on salads range from 4 to 6 per cent in acetic acid content. How much vinegar is too much becomes a matter of taste. Proportions for vinaigrettes, for example, range from the traditional French rubric of one part vinegar to

three parts oil to Elizabeth David's recommendation of one part vinegar to six parts oil.

Wine vinegars are made from red, white and rosé wines, rice wines, sherry and even Champagne. The best wine vinegar comes from France; Orleans, to be precise.

Balsamic vinegar is a remarkable sour/sweet vinegar produced in northern Italy. Aged in a succession of oak, chestnut, mulberry and juniper kegs for at least ten years, its taste and fragrance are incomparable. By Italian law no vinegar not so processed can be called balsamic. Have a bottle of this special vinegar in your cupboard for those times when you want to give your favorite dressings a lift.

1 *Pure olive oil: an inexpensive grade oil.*
2 *Fine olive oil: not to be used for salads.*
3 *Extra virgin olive oil: rare, expensive and heavy.*
4 *Peanut oil: used in South-East Asian cooking.*
5 *Grape seed oil: full-bodied.*
6 *Sunflower seed oil: bland, good for light dressings.*
7 *Walnut oil: aromatic, expensive.*
8 *Hazelnut oil: delicately flavored.*
9 *Sesame oil: mysterious flavor.*

Cider vinegar is produced from apple juice. It is a favorite with Americans as well as health-food devotees.

Malt vinegar is a tart vinegar distilled from malt. Mostly consumed in the United Kingdom, malt vinegar should be used sparingly, since it has a high acetic acid content.

Distilled vinegar is the result of grain distillation. It has no place in salad-making due to its very high acid level. The best use for this vinegar is pickling or household cleaning tasks.

Fruit vinegars are vinegars fermented from fruits such as pears and plums. Their light, fresh flavor makes a wonderful addition to the spectrum of salad dressings. They can be made at home (see page 34) or purchased from specialist food shops.

Herb vinegars are vinegars in which herbs such as basil, rosemary or tarragon have been steeped. Herb vinegars can change an everyday salad dressing into a new taste adventure. They are available commercially or can be made at home (see page 34). Other flavorings added to vinegars include garlic, honey and lemon rind.

VINEGAR HINTS

The party is over and you have a few drops of wine left in several bottles. Don't throw it away. Add the wine to your vinegar; red wine to red vinegar and white wine to white vinegar. The wine will naturally sour in the vinegar bottle and create the impression of an endless supply of vinegar. Don't serve a salad with a vinegar dressing on painted plates. The vinegar will soon corrode the paint on the plates.

1 White wine vinegar.
2 Pure red wine vinegar.
3 Rosemary vinegar: vinegars that
have been steeped in herbs can
transform salad dressings from the
commonplace to the extra special.
4 Lemon wine vinegar: the lemon adds
a lighter touch.
5 French white wine vinegar: the best
wine vinegar comes from Orleans.
6 Raspberry vinegar: adds a light,
fresh flavor to dressings.
7 Cider vinegar.
8 French garlic vinegar.
9 Honey and cider vinegar: a favorite
with health food devotees.
10 Tarragon vinegar: good with white
meat salads.

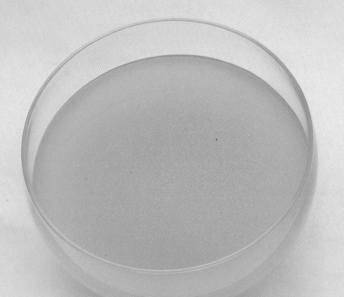

Modern vinaigrette

Mustard vinaigrette

CLASSIC FRENCH VINAIGRETTE

The recipe below is the classic French formula as articulated by generations of haute cuisine *chefs. It calls for oil in a ratio of three to one to the vinegar, and it calls for what to modern taste seems a lot of salt. The oil-to-vinegar proportion should be varied to taste, and the amount of salt can easily be halved.*

MAKES ½ cup

6 tablespoons pure olive oil
2 tablespoons wine vinegar
1 teaspoon salt
⅛ teaspoon freshly ground black pepper

1. Put the vinegar, salt and pepper in a small wooden bowl.
2. Beat with a fork or wire whisk or until the salt dissolves.
3. Add the olive oil and beat until the mixture has a creamy texture.
4. Pour over a mixed green salad and toss gently.

MODERN VINAIGRETTE

Now that you know the classic vinaigrette, try this updated version. Note that it calls for lemon juice and mustard and also requires far less salt. This recipe can easily be halved. it will keep well for up to four days if covered tightly and stored in the refrigerator.

MAKES 1 cup

¾ cup pure olive oil
2 tablespoons wine vinegar
1 tablespoon lemon juice
¼ teaspoon salt, or to taste
⅛ teaspoon freshly ground black pepper

1. Put the vinegar, lemon juice, mustard, salt and pepper in a jar with a tightly fitting lid.
2. Cover the jar tightly and shake until the salt dissolves.
3. Add the olive oil to the jar and shake until well mixed.

FRESH HERB VINEGAR

Fresh herb vinegars add additional depth of flavor to salad dressings, marinades and pickles. Herbs to use include tarragon, basil, rosemary, thyme, whole garlic cloves and coarsely chopped shallots.

MAKES 1 quart

1½ cups fresh herbs
4 cups white or red wine vinegar

1. Wash the herbs and blot them dry. Place in large jar and add the vinegar.
2. Stir well, seal tightly and store the jar in a dark place for 6 weeks. Shake the jar every few days.
3. Strain the vinegar through muslin into smaller bottles. Discard the herbs. Add a few sprigs of fresh herbs to each bottle. Seal the bottles tightly and store them in a dark place.

RASPBERRY VINEGAR

Fruit-flavored vinegars can be made from raspberries, blueberries, black-berries, currants, cherries and pears.

MAKES 2 quarts

8 cups fresh raspberries
1 quart white wine vinegar
3 cups sugar

1. Place 4 cups of the raspberries in a deep jar or bowl. Pour the vinegar over them and let stand for 24 hours.
2. Strain the mixture through a double thickness of clean muslin. Discard the raspberries. Add the remaining 4 cups of raspberries to the strained mixture. Let stand for 24 hours.
3. Strain the mixture through a double thickness of clean muslin. Put the raspberries back into the strained liquid and let stand 24 hours longer. Repeat the straining and standing process twice more, letting the mixture stand for 24 hours each time.
4. Measure the total amount of the strained liquid. Add to it 1 lb of sugar for each ¾ pint of the liquid. Discard the remaining raspberries.

Paprika dressing

Creamy mustard vinaigrette

5. Put the liquid and sugar in a large saucepan and bring to the boil. Boil for 30 minutes, stirring frequently. Remove the mixture from the heat and cool completely. Pour the raspberry vinegar into clean bottles and cork tightly.

PAPRIKA DRESSING

This dressing goes well with any green salad, especially one with mushrooms in it. For a sweeter dressing, add an additional tablespoon of honey or a teaspoon of sugar. This dressing will keep well for three days if tightly covered and refrigerated. It can be halved.

MAKES 1¼ cups

1 tablespoon honey

½ teaspoon salt

1 tablespoon water

2 teaspoons paprika

1 tablespoon Dijon mustard

¼ teaspoon freshy ground black pepper

⅔ cup pure olive oil

4 tablespoons red wine vinegar

1. Put the honey, salt and water in a jar with tightly fitting lid. Cover the jar tightly and shake until the honey and salt dissolve.
2. Add the paprika, mustard and pepper. Shake well.
3. Add the oil and vinegar. Shake until all the ingredients are combined.

MUSTARD VINAIGRETTE

In this tangy version of vinaigrette, soy sauce substitutes for most of the salt and the mustard gives bite. This dressing is excellent over a simple salad of lettuce, tomato and avocado.

MAKES ½ cup

5 tablespoons pure olive oil

2 tablespoons red wine vinegar

1 tablespoon Dijon mustard

½ teaspoon dried thyme

1½ teaspoons soy sauce

¼ teaspoon salt

¼ teaspoon freshly ground black pepper

1. Put the olive oil, vinegar and mustard in a wooden bowl. Stir with a fork until somewhat foamy.
2. Stir in the thyme and soy sauce.
3. Add the salt and pepper. Stir well and pour over salad.

YOGURT VINAIGRETTE

In this version of vinaigrette, the oil is replaced by yogurt and the vinegar by lemon juice. Serve it over a green salad.

MAKES 3½ fl oz/100 ml

2 fl oz/60 ml unflavoured yogurt

4 teaspoons fresh lemon juice

1 tablespoon/15 ml Dijon mustard

½ teaspoon dried thyme

1½ teaspoons soy sauce

¼ teaspoon salt

¼ teaspoon freshly ground black pepper

1. Put the yogurt, lemon juice and mustard in a small bowl. Stir with a fork or whisk until the mixture is somewhat foamy.
2. Stir in the thyme, soy sauce, salt and pepper.

CREAMY MUSTARD VINAIGRETTE

This variation on mustard vinaigrette goes well over any green salad. It's also good over steamed asparagus. Use the dressing within an hour of making it.

MAKES ½ cup

3 tablespoons olive oil

2 tablespoons heavy cream

2 tablespoons red wine vinegar

1 tablespoon Dijon mustard

½ teaspoon dried thyme

1½ teaspoons soy sauce

¼ teaspoon salt

¼ teaspoon freshly ground black pepper

1. Put the olive oil, cream, vinegar and mustard in a small bowl. Stir with a fork or whisk until the mixture is somewhat foamy.
2. Stir in the thyme, soy sauce, salt and pepper.

CHINESE DRESSING

Oyster sauce has a subtle but definite presence in this dressing. A teaspoon of dried basil or ground ginger will add an exotic flavor. Use Chinese Dressing over mixed green salads or steamed vegetables. The dressing will keep well in a tightly covered container in the refrigerator for three days.

MAKES 1 cup

2 teaspoons soy sauce

2 teaspoons oyster sauce

2 teaspoons water

1 garlic clove, finely chopped

¼ teaspoon dried basil

¾ cup peanut oil

7 teaspoons rice wine vinegar

1. In a jar with a tightly fitting lid, put the soy sauce, oyster sauce, water, garlic and basil. Cover and shake until the ingredients are blended. Allow to stand for 3 minutes.
2. Add the peanut oil and vinegar to the jar, cover and shake well again.

BUTTERMILK DRESSING

The buttermilk sold today is artificially soured skimmed milk. Nonetheless, it makes a good dressing. For a lighter version of this dressing, use a scant ½ cup of buttermilk and replace the cottage cheese with 2 teaspoons of olive oil. Try substituting dried chervil, parsley or summer savory for the dill. Do not halve the recipe. Buttermilk Dressing will keep well for up to two days in the refrigerator if tightly covered. It goes well with tomatoes, cucumber and green salads.

MAKES 1 cup

½ cup cultured buttermilk

¼ cup cottage cheese

1 tablespoon finely chopped onion

3 tablespoons lemon juice

1 teaspoon dried dill

¼ teaspoon salt

1. Put all the ingredients in a blender and blend well. To make by hand, put all the ingredients in a bowl and stir with a wire whisk until well blended.
2. Serve.

CORIANDER DRESSING

To use fresh coriander instead of dried in this recipe, substitute 1½ tablespoons chopped fresh coriander for the 1½ teaspoons dried. Let the dressing stand at room temperature for 20 minutes before using. Coriander Dressing is very good on green salads. To serve it with steamed vegetables, pour the dressing over the vegetables and let them marinate for at least 30 minutes before serving. This recipe is easily halved. It will keep well in the refrigerator for three days.

MAKES 1¼ cups

1½ teaspoons dried coriander

½ teaspoon dried basil

½ teaspoon dried chives

1 tablespoon water

1 teaspoon Dijon-style mustard

1 garlic clove, finely chopped

¾ cup peanut oil

3 tablespoons tarragon vinegar

⅛ teaspoon salt

1. Put the coriander, basil, chives and water in a jar with a tightly fitting lid. Cover and shake well for 15 seconds.
2. Add the mustard and garlic to the jar. Cover tightly and shake well again. Allow to stand for 5 minutes.
3. Add the oil, vinegar and salt to the jar. Cover tightly and shake again for 15 seconds.

FRENCH GARDEN DRESSING

Everything in this dressing must be fresh, fresh, fresh! It's wonderful with seafood salads or crudités. Try it on cold roast meat or poultry. This recipe should not be halved. If tightly covered, it will keep in the refrigerator for two days.

Buttermilk dressing

Coriander dressing

MAKES 1¾ cups

¼ cup extra virgin olive oil

5 tablespoons tarragon vinegar

1 garlic clove, finely chopped

¼ cup tomatoes, seeded and chopped

2 teaspoons chopped fresh basil

1 teaspoon Dijon-style mustard

1 tablespoon chopped green pepper

1 tablespoon chopped fresh parsley

1 tablespoon chopped onion

¼ teaspoon salt

¼ teaspoon freshly ground black pepper

½ cup pure olive oil

1. Put all the ingredients except for the pure olive oil in a blender. Blend until everything combines and the oil emulsifies, about 10 seconds.
2. Add the remaining olive oil and blend for only 3 seconds. Mix well before serving.

SOUR CREAM DRESSING

Like mayonnaise, sour cream makes an excellent base for salad dressings. For a sweet dressing for fruit salads, leave out the mustard and paprika and add 3 tablespoons honey or 4 tablespoons fresh orange juice.

MAKES 1⅓ cups

2 tablespoons sugar

3 tablespoons fresh lemon juice

1 teaspoon Dijon-style mustard

¼ teaspoon paprika

½ teaspoon salt

freshly ground black pepper

1 cup sour cream

1. Mix the sugar, lemon juice, mustard, paprika, salt and pepper together in a bowl.
2. Add the sour cream. Stir slowly until well mixed. Chill before serving.

LEMON DRESSING

This tart dressing is best over such steamed vegetables as asparagus, green peas, broccoli or cauliflower. It may be stored for two days in a tightly covered container in the refrigerator. The recipe should not be halved.

MAKES ¾ cup

1 teaspoon water

⅛ teaspoon salt

⅛ teaspoon grated lemon rind

2 teaspoons dried mint

2 fl oz/60 ml fresh lemon juice

4 tablespoons fresh lemon juice

½ cup pure olive oil

1. Put the water, salt and lemon rind in a jar with a tightly fitting lid. Let stand for 2 minutes.

2. Add the mint and lemon juice. Cover the jar tightly and shake.
3. Add the olive oil and black pepper. Cover the jar tightly, shake again and serve.

TOUCH OF ASIA DRESSING

This dressing adds zest to a simple lettuce salad. Store, tightly covered, in the refrigerator for up to two days.

MAKES 1½ cups

2 teaspoons soy sauce

2 teaspoons water

1 whole green onion, chopped

½ teaspoon sesame oil

¼ teaspoon hot pepper chili oil

1 garlic clove, finely chopped

¼ teaspoon ground black pepper

¾ cup peanut oil

7 teaspoons rice wine vinegar

1. Put the soy sauce, water, green onion, sesame oil, hot pepper oil, garlic and black pepper in a jar with a tightly fitting lid. Cover and shake until the ingredients are blended.
2. Add the peanut oil to the jar, cover tightly and shake again. Let the mixture stand for 2 minutes.
3. Add the vinegar to the jar. Cover tightly and shake well again. Pour over the salad immediately.

French garden dressing

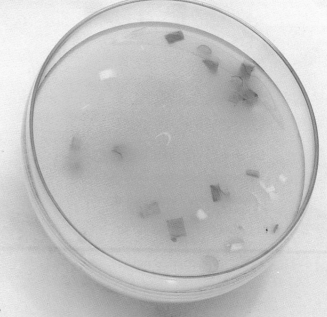

Touch of Asia dressing

NATIVE AMERICAN DRESSING

This dressing is good on salads that include chicory (escarole), dandelion leaves and spinach. The recipe can be halved. Make it fresh shortly before serving as it does not store well.

MAKES 1¼ cups

1 cup Modern Vinaigrette (see page 34)

2 hard-cooked egg yolks, mashed

1 garlic clove, finely chopped

1 tablespoon finely chopped parsley

1 tablespoon finely chopped green pepper

1 tablespoon finely chopped sweet red pepper

1 tablespoon chopped green onion

1. Put the French dressing and the mashed egg yolks in a jar with a tightly fitting lid. Shake well.
2. Add the remaining ingredients to the jar and shake vigorously until well mixed.

JAPANESE DRESSING

Because curry powder does not store well when combined with liquids, this dressing (also containing dashi, *a Japanese flavoring made from dried bonito fish) should be stored in the refrigerator, covered, for no more than two days. Serve with mixed greens.*

MAKES 1 cup

1½ teaspoons instant dashi

1 tablespoon hot water

1 teaspoon honey

1 garlic clove, finely chopped

¼ teaspoon curry powder

1 teaspoon dried tarragon

¾ cup pure olive oil or peanut oil

3 tablespoons tarragon vinegar

1. Put the *dashi* and hot water in a jar with a tightly fitting lid. Stir until the *dashi* is completely dissolved.
2. Add the honey and garlic. Cover the jar tightly and shake until the

honey is dissolved.
3. Add the curry powder and tarragon. Cover jar and shake well.
4. Add the oil and vinegar. Shake.
5. Let stand for 5 minutes, shake well and pour over salad.

CURRY MAYONNAISE I

Curry powder is usually made from some or all of the following ground and dried ingredients: cumin, turmeric, coriander, ginger, black pepper, cardamom, fennel, chili, peppers, mace, cloves, mustard and poppy seeds. The proportions vary from cook to cook. This version of Curry Mayonnaise is particularly good with chicken or shrimp salad. It can be stored in a tightly covered container in the refrigerator for three days; do not halve the recipe.

MAKES 1¼ cups

1 cup mayonnaise

2 teaspoons curry powder

1 teaspoon tarragon vinegar

1 small garlic clove, finely chopped

1. Prepare the basic mayonnaise, adding 1 teaspoon of curry powder to egg mixture before stirring in the oil.
2. Add the vinegar, garlic and the remaining teaspoon of curry powder to the mayonnaise. Mix thoroughly.

CURRY MAYONNAISE II

This very flavorful version of Curry Mayonnaise goes well with raw vegetables, especially cauliflower. It also makes a very interesting potato salad. As with the previous version, this dressing can be stored in a tightly covered container in the refrigerator for three days; do not halve the recipe.

MAKES 1⅓ cups

1 cup mayonnaise

2 teaspoons curry powder

3 tablespoons heavy cream

1. When making the basic mayonnaise, add 1 teaspoon of curry

powder to the egg mixture before adding the oil.
2. Stir the heavy cream and the remaining teaspoon of curry powder into the finished mayonnaise.

CREAMY DRESSING

This all-purpose dressing goes well with green salads, steamed vegetables and tortellini salad. If tightly covered and refrigerated, Creamy Dressing will keep well for two days. Do not halve the recipe.

MAKES ½ cup

2 tablespoons wine vinegar

6 tablespoons pure olive oil

1 teaspoon salt

½ teaspoon freshly ground black pepper

2 teaspoons Dijon-style mustard

2 garlic cloves, finely chopped

2 teaspoons crème fraîche *or sour cream*

1. Put all the ingredients except for the *crème fraîche* in a jar with a tightly fitting lid. Cover jar and shake well.
2. Add the *crème fraîche* to the jar. Cover the jar tightly and shake until well blended.

PINK MAYONNAISE

Pink Mayonnaise is good with cold vegetable salads. It also adds extra flavor to tuna or chicken salads. The recipe may be halved; it should be stored in a tightly covered container in the refrigerator for up to three days.

MAKES 1½ cups

1 cup mayonnaise

4 tablespoons tomato paste

4 tablespoons pimento, finely chopped

½ teaspoon fresh lemon juice

½ teaspoon Worcestershire sauce

1 small garlic clove, finely chopped

1. Mix the mayonnaise and tomato paste in a bowl until well blended.
2. Add the pimento, lemon juice, Worcestershire sauce and garlic. Blend well.

TOFU MAYONNAISE

Tofu Mayonnaise can be used whenever a recipe calls for mayonnaise. It will keep well in the refrigerator in a tightly covered container for three days.

MAKES 2½ cups

1 egg yolk

1 teaspoon dry mustard

2 cakes tofu (bean curd), cut into small cubes

¼ cup safflower or light vegetable oil

7 tablespoons unflavored yogurt

2 tablespoons lemon juice

1 tablespoon white wine vinegar

½ teaspoon salt

1. Put the egg yolk and mustard in a blender. Blend for 3 to 5 seconds.
2. Add the tofu and safflower oil. Blend for 10 seconds.
3. Add the yogurt, lemon juice, vinegar and salt. Blend until the mixture has a creamy texture.

CREAM MAYONNAISE

A creamier, lighter version of mayonnaise, this dressing should be used with green salads or salads of tomato and cucumber. Never use it with a salad containing onions. For an interesting variation, add 2 tablespoons of chopped pimento (sweet red peppers preserved in cans or jars). Cream Mayonnaise will keep in the refrigerator for two days if tightly covered.

MAKES 1½ cups

½ cup whipping cream

1 cup mayonnaise

salt to taste

freshly ground black pepper to taste

1. Whip the cream until it is stiff but not dry.
2. Put the mayonnaise in a medium-sized bowl. Slowly fold in the whipped cream.
4. Add salt and pepper to taste. Mix together well.

CRÈME FRAÎCHE

Use only fresh heavy cream. Crème fraîche should be refrigerated for at least 12 hours before serving. It will keep well in the refrigerator for five to seven days if it is tightly covered.

MAKES 1 cup

1 cup heavy cream

1 to 2 tablespoons buttermilk

1. Combine the heavy cream and the buttermilk (the more buttermilk the tangier the flavor) in a jar with a tightly fitting lid. Cover the jar tightly and shake until the ingredients are well combined, about 1 to 2 minutes.
2. Let the jar stand at room temperature overnight or until the mixture is thick.

YOGURT MAYONNAISE

This is good with fruit salads, bean sprout salads, and salads of chicory (escarole), or Chinese cabbage. Make fresh before using; it does not store well.

MAKES 1 cup

½ cup unflavored yogurt

1 tablespoon honey

1 teaspoon fresh lemon juice

⅓ cup mayonnaise

¼ teaspoon salt

1 teaspoon poppy seeds

1. Combine the yogurt, honey and lemon juice in a bowl. Stir with a wooden spoon until well blended.
2. Add the mayonnaise, salt and poppy seeds. Stir until thoroughly mixed. Chill for 1 hour and serve.

AÏOLI

This garlic mayonnaise is traditionally served with cooked vegetables, seafood and boiled potatoes.

MAKES 1⅓ cups

4 garlic cloves

½ teaspoon salt

2 egg yolks

½ teaspoon Tabasco sauce

1 tablespoon lemon juice

1 cup pure olive oil

1 tablespoon white wine vinegar

½ teaspoon ground black pepper

1. Mash the garlic and salt to a paste.
2. Transfer the garlic paste to a small mixing bowl. Add the egg yolks and Tabasco sauce. Beat with a wire whisk until blended. Beat in lemon juice.
3. Beat in ½ cup of the olive oil, a drop at a time.
4. Beat in the remaining olive oil, 1 tablespoon at a time.
5. Add the vinegar and black pepper and beat until well blended.

GREEN MAYONNAISE

Fish salads or raw vegetables are good with this dressing. Green Mayonnaise will keep well in the refrigerator for three days if tightly covered. Do not halve the recipe.

MAKES 1⅔ cups

3 tablespoons chopped fresh spinach

3 tablespoons chopped watercress

3 tablespoons chopped green onion

3 tablespoons chopped parsley

1 cup mayonnaise

⅛ teaspoon grated nutmeg

salt to taste

1. Put the spinach, watercress, green onion and parsley in a small saucepan. Add water to cover them.
2. Quickly bring to the boil. Remove the saucepan from the heat. Let stand for 1 minute.
3. Drain the greens well. Rub them through a sieve or purée them in a blender. Drain off excess liquid.
4. Put the mayonnaise in a blender or medium-sized bowl. Add the purée, nutmeg and salt to taste. Blend until evenly mixed.

Herb dressing　　　　　　　　　　　**Italian dressing**

HERB DRESSING

When fresh herbs are available, substitute 1½ teaspoons chopped fresh chives for dried, and/or 1½ teaspoons chopped fresh chervil for dried. For a creamy herb dressing add 1 tablespoon heavy cream and use 1 tablespoon less olive oil. This dressing is very good with green salads, especially those containing peas. It can be stored, tightly covered, for three days in the refrigerator; it is easily halved.

MAKES 1 cup

1 tablespoon water
½ teaspoon salt
½ teaspoon dried chives
½ teaspoon dried chervil
½ teaspoon dried summer savory
¼ teaspoon freshly ground black pepper
1 teaspoon chopped green onion
1 tablespoon chopped fresh parsley
½ cup pure olive oil
3 tablespoons tarragon vinegar

1. Put the water in a jar with a tightly fitting lid and add the salt, chives, chervil and summer savory. Let stand for 5 minutes.
2. Add the pepper, green onion and parsley. Cover the jar tightly and shake well. Let stand for 2 minutes.
3. Add the oil and vinegar to the jar. Cover tightly and shake well. Pour over the salad immediately.

ITALIAN DRESSING

For the best results, don't economize — use extra virgin olive oil and balsamic vinegar where they are called for. This dressing is Italian, so of course it's perfect on antipasto or over a green salad served with a pasta main course. The recipe may be halved. It will keep in the refrigerator for three days if kept tightly covered.

MAKES 1⅓ cups

1 tablespoon water
1 teaspoon dried basil
¼ teaspoon salt
¼ teaspoon dried oregano
1 whole green onion, finely chopped
2 tablespoons balsamic vinegar
2 tablespoons red wine vinegar
½ cup virgin or extra virgin olive oil
¼ cup pure olive oil

1. Put the water, basil, salt, oregano and green onion in a jar with a tightly fitting lid. Close the jar tightly, shake well and let stand for 5 minutes.
2. Add the vinegars. Shake the covered jar again.
3. Add the oils, shake and serve.

ROQUEFORT SOUR CREAM DRESSING

This dressing is good over any green salad, especially where iceberg lettuce is used. It should be used immediately. Do not halve the recipe.

MAKES 1½ cups

¼ teaspoon cayenne pepper
¼ teaspoon salt
freshly ground black pepper to taste
2 teaspoons cider vinegar
1 cup sour cream
½ cup Roquefort cheese, crumbled

1. Combine the cayenne pepper, salt, pepper and vinegar in a bowl. Stir until the salt dissolves.
2. Stir in the sour cream. Add the Roquefort cheese and mix well. Chill for at least 1 hour before serving.

ALL-PURPOSE DRESSING

Try it on green salads, with tuna or potato salad, or over steamed vegetables. Add a teaspoon of curry powder and try it over spinach salad. Liquid seasoning is available from delicatessens and oriental food shops.

MAKES 1 cup

⅔ cup pure olive oil
¼ cup tarragon vinegar
2 teaspoons liquid seasoning

Homemade mayonnaise

Russian dressing

| 1 teaspoon sugar |
| 1/2 teaspoon salt |
| 1/4 teaspoon pepper |
| 1 garlic clove, finely chopped |
| 1 egg |

1. Put all the ingredients in a jar with a tightly fitting lid. Close the jar tightly and shake until the ingredients are well blended.
2. Serve.

HOMEMADE MAYONNAISE

There are two inviolable rules for making mayonnaise successfully: the eggs must be at room temperature and the oil must be added very, very slowly. The flavor of the mayonnaise depends on the type and quality of oil used, not the tartness of the lemon juice or vinegar.

Using the basic recipe below, a number of flavored mayonnaises can be made. To make garlic mayonnaise, add 1 or 2 crushed garlic cloves for each egg yolk (see the recipe on page 39). For a delicious and colorful mayonnaise, add 1/8 teaspoon of crushed dried thyme and 2 teaspoons of tomato paste. When fresh herbs are available, for each egg yolk add 2 tablespoons of finely chopped fresh tarragon, basil, parsley, chives, watercress or other herbs.

If the mayonnaise seems too thick, beat in an additional teaspoon of vinegar or lemon juice.

To keep mayonnaise from separating if it is made more than an hour in advance, beat 1 tablespoon boiling water into the mixture.

Should the mayonnaise separate, it can still be rescued. Try beating in a teaspoon of boiling water. If that fails, beat an egg yolk in a clean bowl. Slowly add the separated mayonnaise to the egg yolk, beating continuously.

Mayonnaise can be stored for at least a week in a tightly covered container in the refrigerator. Do not attempt to halve the recipe.

MAKES 1 1/4 cups

| 2 egg yolks |
| 1 teaspoon dry mustard |
| 1/2 teaspoon salt |
| 1/8 teaspoon cayenne pepper |
| 1 cup pure olive oil |
| 2 tablespoons lemon juice or wine vinegar |

1. Beat the egg yolks, dry mustard, salt and cayenne pepper in a bowl, using either wire whisk or a fork, until thick. Either beat by hand or use an electric beater at the setting used for whipping cream.
2. Slowly and carefully add the oil, a drop at a time, while beating the egg yolk mixture continuously, until you have mixed in 1/2 cup of the oil.
3. Beat for a minute or two longer. The mayonnaise will thicken.

4. Resume beating, adding 2 tablespoons of the oil and 1 teaspoon of vinegar or lemon juice at a time, until all the oil and vinegar or lemon juice are used. Stop beating when the mayonnaise is as thick as whipped cream.

RUSSIAN DRESSING

Any lettuce salad goes well with Russian Dressing. It's also a great dressing for turkey or roast beef sandwiches. For a more authentic Russian flavor, add 1 tablespoon of chopped fresh dill. This dressing can be stored, tightly covered, in the refrigerator for four days.

MAKES 1 1/2 cups

| 1 cup mayonnaise |
| 1 tablespoon tomato paste |
| 1 tablespoon red wine vinegar |
| 2 tablespoons chili or Tabasco sauce |
| 1 tablespoon finely chopped celery |
| 1 tablespoon finely chopped onion |
| 3 tablespoons caviar or lumpfish roe |
| 1 tablespoon sour cream |
| 1 teaspoon Worcestershire sauce |
| salt to taste |

1. Combine all the ingredients and mix well together. A blender will do just as well as a bowl with a wooden spoon.
2. Serve.

THOUSAND ISLAND DRESSING

This recipe for Thousand Island Dressing is so flavorful and rich that it sometimes overwhelms those accustomed to the bottled versions. Serve it with any lettuce salad, especially iceberg lettuce. It will keep in the refrigerator, covered, for three days; the recipe may be halved.

MAKES 1¾ cups

1 cup mayonnaise

¼ cup Tabasco or chili sauce

2 tablespoons minced pimento-stuffed green olives

1 hard-cooked egg, finely chopped

1 tablespoon heavy cream

½ teaspoon fresh lemon juice

1½ teaspoons finely chopped green onion

2 tablespoons finely chopped green pepper

2 tablespoons finely chopped fresh parsley

¼ teaspoon paprika

⅛ teaspoon freshly ground black pepper

1. Put the mayonnaise and chili sauce in a medium-sized bowl. Stir with a wooden spoon until well blended.
2. Add the olives, egg, cream and lemon juice. Continue stirring.
3. Add the remaining ingredients. Stir until well blended. Refrigerate for at least 1 hour before serving.

BOILED DRESSING

Although it must be cooked in a double boiler, the honest flavor of Boiled Dressing is definitely worth the trouble, especially when used with potato salad or cole-slaw. The recipe cannot be halved. Boiled Dressing will keep well in a tightly covered container in the refrigerator for five days.

MAKES 1⅓ cups

2 tablespoons sugar

2 tablespoons flour

½ teaspoon salt

¾ teaspoon dry mustard

⅛ teaspoon paprika

1 cup milk

2 egg yolks, beaten

3 tablespoons cider vinegar

2 tablespoons melted butter

1. Half fill the bottom of a double boiler with water. Bring to the boil.
2. In the top half of the double boiler, before putting it over the heat, combine the sugar, flour, salt, mustard and paprika. Mix well. Slowly add the milk, stirring constantly.
3. Place the top half of the double boiler over the boiling water. Continue to stir. When the mixture begins to thicken, add the egg yolks, vinegar and melted butter, always stirring constantly.
4. Cook, stirring constantly, until the dressing is thick.
5. Remove the double boiler from the heat. Transfer the dressing to a small bowl and chill before serving.

EGG DRESSING

This rich delicious dressing is best over green salads. The whites from the hard-cooked eggs can be used to garnish the salad. The dressing should be made just before use; it cannot be stored.

MAKES ¾ cup

3 tablespoons white wine vinegar

½ teaspoon dry mustard

⅛ teaspoon sugar

⅛ teaspoon cayenne pepper

3 hard-cooked egg yolks

2 egg yolks, lightly beaten

⅓ cup cream

2 tablespoons sour cream

Thousand Island dressing

Boiled dressing

2 tablespoons chopped fresh chives or 2 teaspoons dried chives

¼ teaspoon salt

¼ teaspoon freshly ground black pepper

1. In a small bowl mix the vinegar, mustard, sugar, and cayenne pepper until a paste is formed.
2. Rub the hard-cooked egg yolks through a sieve into a bowl. Add the uncooked egg yolks to the hard-cooked egg yolks. Stir until blended.
3. Stirring continuously, add the cream, then the vinegar and mustard paste mixture, then the sour cream, then the chives and then the salt and pepper. Stir well after each addition.

HONEY FRUIT MAYONNAISE

This sweet mayonnaise dressing can be used on melon and fruit salads, as a dip for fresh fruit or, sparingly, on lettuce salads. It may be halved; store it in a tightly covered container in the refrigerator for up to three days.

MAKES 1⅔ cups

1 cup Homemade Mayonnaise (see page 41)

½ cup honey

---

1 tablespoon fresh orange juice

2 tablespoons grated lemon rind

1. Place the mayonnaise and honey in a bowl. Mix well, using a wooden spoon, electric beater or blender.
2. Add the orange juice and lemon rind. Continue mixing until smooth. Chill for 1 hour before serving.

SWEET YOGURT DRESSING

This dressing comes from California, where the state vegetable is the bean sprout. For a dieter's lunch, try a small head of any soft lettuce and ¼ cup of this dressing. The recipe is easily halved; the dressing will keep, tightly covered, in the refrigerator for three days.

MAKES 1⅓ cups

2 tablespoons honey

3 tablespoons white wine vinegar

1 cup unflavored yogurt

1 teaspoon celery or poppy seeds

1 teaspoon prepared mustard

1. Put the honey and vinegar in a bowl. Stir until honey dissolves.
2. Add the yogurt, celery or poppy seeds and mustard. Mix well. Chill for 1 hour before serving.

FRUIT SALAD SYRUP DRESSING

An all-purpose dressing for fresh fruit salads, this recipe goes particularly well with pineapple, grapes, oranges, grapefruit and apples. Use the dressing within a short time of making it.

MAKES 1¼ cups

1 tablespoon flour

2 tablespoons water

½ teaspoon pure vanilla extract

1 egg

½ cup sugar

½ cup water

2 teaspoons butter

⅛ teaspoon ground nutmeg

3 tablespoons heavy cream

1. Put the flour and 2 tablespoons water into a saucepan. Stir to form a thin paste. Add the vanilla and egg. Beat well until smooth.
2. Put the sugar, ½ cup water and butter in another saucepan. Bring to the boil over a low heat.
3. Add the boiling syrup to the vanilla and egg mixture. Stir well. Cook over low heat, stirring constantly, until thick and smooth.
4. Remove the saucepan from the heat. Allow the dressing to cool.
5. Stir in the nutmeg and cream.

Egg dressing

Fruit salad syrup dressing

SAL

Salads are a
be simple or
starter or a
offers a wide selection of
vegetable salads, bean
pasta salads, rice salads
salads. In short, a salad

ADS

moveable feast; they can

elaborate, a side dish, a

main course. This section

recipes for green salads,

salads, seafood salads,

meat salads and fruit

for every season...

Recipes for Salads

That salads are by no means limited to 'rabbit food' can be seen by the recipes in this chapter which range from meat, poultry and pasta salads to bean, seafood and fruit ones.

Whether serving a salad as a starter, main course or dessert, you will find an appropriate recipe here. Remember that since cold food doesn't entice by smell, presentation is of vital importance.

GREEN AND VEGETABLE SALADS

Almost any vegetable can be used in a salad. The only requirement is that the vegetable be fresh. Try to buy locally grown produce when possible. Always buy vegetables when they are in season. Those bought out of season have often been forced or treated and will be less than flavorful.

The freshest type of vegetable salad, and one of the easiest to prepare, is *crudités*. These are simply crisp raw vegetables, such as cauliflower florets, radishes, green pepper strips and carrot sticks, artfully arranged on a serving platter and served with a dip that acts as a dressing. Some good choices for a dip are Aïoli (see page 39), Tarama Salad (see page 65) and Nam Prik Pak (see page 65). Roquefort Sour Cream Dressing (see page 40) and French Garden Dressing (see page 36) are also good.

BEAN SALADS

Since prehistoric times beans have been an important source of nutrition. We now know that beans are high in protein and complex carbohydrates and low in calories and fat — and that they are delicious. Beans seem to lend themselves well to salads. Cannellini (white kidney) beans and chick peas are all popular choices.

Soaked and cooked dried beans are preferable to canned beans. They will have better flavor and texture. When cooking dried beans, do not use the soaking liquid, use fresh water instead. Add 1/8 teaspoon of baking soda to the water to prevent the beans from becoming musty. To see if the beans are done, remove a few from the pan and blow on them. If the skin pops or splits, the beans are ready.

SEAFOOD SALADS

Fish consumption is on the rise as health-conscious eaters have become increasingly aware of the low fat and calorie content of fish.

When buying fish, always seek out the freshest possible. Look for fish that are firm to the touch. The fish should not be dull in color or have a very fishy or unpleasant odor. When cooking shellfish, discard any that do not open when the rest have.

If possible, use fresh, uncooked shrimp, not frozen. They should be cooked in their shells until they are a bright pink color. Remove the vein that runs down the back of the shrimp with a sharp knife.

True lobsters have large claws. Spiny lobsters, also known as rock lobsters, sea crayfish or langouste, have no claws but do have a spiny shell. Lobsters should be bought live if possible.

PASTA AND GRAIN SALADS

Pasta salads are a relatively recent development in salad-making. Pasta should be cooked *al dente*, which means literally 'to the tooth'. To do this, cook the pasta in a large pan of boiling salted water until it is just tender but still slightly resistant to the bite. Drain it well; or the pasta salad will be watery.

Pasta comes in a multitude of shapes and sizes — spirals, bows, wheels, shells, tubes may all be used.

MEAT AND POULTRY SALADS

Leftover beef, veal, lamb or pork are all easily re-used in meat salads. Leftover poultry, too, can be used. The poultry in these recipes can often be interchanged. For example, any chicken salad recipe is just as good when made with leftover turkey or veal. It is very easy to cook chicken quickly for use in a salad. Simply poach the chicken pieces in simmering chicken broth for 20 to 25 minutes.

FRUIT SALADS

Fruit salads generally fall into two categories: side salads and desserts. Fruit side salads are usually combined with nuts and cheeses of various sorts. Dessert salads are made almost exclusively with fruit. The dressings for fruit salads range from sweetened vinaigrettes to yogurt or sour cream bases. An elegant after-dinner fruit salad can be made by marinating fresh fruit pieces in fruit-flavored liqueurs or Champagne. Prepare fruit salads shortly before use or they may discolor.

It is very important to toss the salad so that each leaf is coated in the dressing. Delicate fresh green salad leaves should be tossed just before serving as they wilt if left sitting in a dressing. The more robust green and root vegetables can be dressed in advance and it is often a good idea to do this anyway because by marinating them for a while, they will develop a better flavor.

Caesar Salad

INGREDIENTS/TO SERVE 6–8

2 large heads romaine (cos) lettuce

1 garlic clove, finely chopped

½ cup pure olive oil

½ teaspoon freshly ground black pepper

½ teaspoon salt

2 tablespoons fresh lemon juice

½ cup freshly grated Parmesan cheese

6 to 8 anchovy fillets

¼ teaspoon Worcestershire sauce

2 eggs (raw or hard-cooked)

1½ cups Garlic Croûtons (see below)

● Photograph opposite (before adding eggs)

Not a salad in the tradition of Julius, Rome, 48 BC, but in the tradition of Caesar Cardini, Tiajuana, circa 1920. Cardini was a restaurateur; his salad has now won international acclaim.

1. Pull the lettuce leaves from the stalks and tear them into large but still bite-sized pieces or use small whole leaves.
2. Put the garlic and olive oil in a jar with a tightly fitting lid. Cover and shake well. Set the jar aside.
3. Put the lettuce in a large salad bowl. Put each of the other ingredients into its own small bowl.
4. In front of your guests, grind the pepper over the lettuce leaves with a pepper mill. Add the olive oil and toss to coat the lettuce.
5. Sprinkle the lettuce with salt. Add the lemon juice, Parmesan cheese, anchovy fillets and Worcestershire sauce to the lettuce. Toss, twice, gently.
6. Break the eggs into the salad. Toss gently.
7. Add the croûtons, toss and serve.

Garlic Croûtons

INGREDIENTS

1 garlic clove, finely chopped

¾ cup pure olive oil

2 cups fresh bread, cubed

These can be stored for a few days in an airtight container, but it is far better to make only what you need shortly before you need it.

1. Put the garlic and olive oil in a jar with a tightly fitting lid. Cover tightly and shake well. Let stand for several hours.
2. Heat the garlic and olive oil in a skillet. Add the bread cubes. Cook, turning frequently, until the cubes are browned.
3. Remove the cubes from the pan and drain on paper towels.

Pine Nuts and Watercress

INGREDIENTS/TO SERVE 4

¼ cup pine nuts

2 large bunches watercress

¾ cup fresh parsley, finely chopped

½ cup fresh chives, finely chopped

¾ cup Lemon Dressing (see page 37)

Once the pine nuts (pignoli) in this recipe have been toasted, they can be stored in a small plastic bag and frozen for later use.

1. Preheat the oven to 350°F/180°C/mark 4.
2. Put the pine nuts on a baking sheet and toast them in the oven until browned, about 8 to 10 minutes.
3. Put the watercress, parsley and chives in a salad bowl. Add the Lemon Dressing and toss. Add the pine nuts and toss again.

Orange and Mixed Green Salad

INGREDIENTS/TO SERVE 4

½ head chicory (escarole) or Boston lettuce

2 large navel oranges

1 cup carrots, cut in strips

¼ cup sultanas or currants

¾ cup Paprika Dressing (see page 35)

● Photograph opposite

Refreshing in sight and taste, this salad is an excellent accompaniment to roast lamb or pork. Serve it with a dry white wine.

1. Tear the lettuce into bite-sized pieces. Arrange them in a salad bowl.
2. Peel the oranges and divide them into segments. Cut each segment into halves or thirds. Add the pieces to the salad bowl.
3. Add the carrots and sultanas to the salad bowl and toss.
4. Add the Paprika Dressing and toss.

Garden Mixed Green Salad

INGREDIENTS/TO SERVE 6–8

1 head Boston lettuce or garden lettuce

1 medium-sized head romaine (cos) lettuce

3 Belgian endives

¼ cup celery, chopped

3 hard-cooked eggs, sliced

½ cup watercress, thick stems removed, coarsely chopped

½ medium-sized onion, sliced into rings

2 large tomatoes, peeled and cut in wedges

½ cup pickled beets, cut in strips

2 tablespoons fresh parsley, chopped

1⅓ cups French Dressing (see page 34)

Almost any fresh salad green may be substituted for those called for here. This salad goes well with beef or veal roasts. It is also substantial enough to be served alone, along with a bottle of Chianti or Zinfandel, as a light lunch or supper. Try using Native American Dressing (see page 38) or Coriander Dressing (see page 36) instead of the French Dressing.

1. Line the salad bowl with some leaves of the Boston or garden lettuce.
2. Tear the remaining Boston lettuce and the cos lettuce into bite-sized pieces. Add them to the salad bowl.
3. Cut the endives into bite-sized pieces. Add them to the salad bowl.
4. Add the celery, eggs, watercress, onion rings and tomatoes to the salad bowl. Toss gently. Refrigerate until ready to serve.
5. Before serving, add the beets, parsley and French Dressing. Toss and serve.

Mixed Greens and Mushrooms
with Raspberry Vinaigrette

The raspberry vinaigrette and toasted pine nuts are the ingredients that make this salad extra special.

1. Preheat the oven to 350°F/180°C/Gas Mark 4.
2. Place the pine nuts in a shallow baking dish and toast them in the oven until lightly browned, about 5 minutes. Remove from oven and set aside.
3. Wash and gently dry the Boston lettuce, endives and radicchio.
4. Tear the lettuce and radicchio into bite-sized pieces. Cut the endive into thin slices. Put the greens into a large salad bowl. Add the mushrooms and toasted pine nuts.
5. In a mixing bowl combine the olive oil, vinegar, shallot, mustard, cream, salt and pepper. Whisk until the vinaigrette is smooth and well blended.
6. Pour the vinaigrette over the greens and toss well. Serve at once.

INGREDIENTS/TO SERVE 4

½ cup pine nuts (pignoli)

2 heads Boston lettuce or other soft lettuce

2 Belgian endives

1 small head radicchio

¼ cup stemmed small mushrooms

Raspberry Vinaigrette:

4 tablespoons olive oil

2 tablespoons raspberry vinegar

1 finely chopped shallot

1 teaspoon Dijon-style mustard

2 teaspoons heavy cream

salt to taste, if desired

freshly ground black pepper to taste

● *Photograph opposite, above*

Endive Salad

A perfect salad for before or after the main course, Endive Salad calls for prosciutto, a type of Italian ham. It has a nutty flavor that is both salty and peppery — and unique.

1. Cut the endives diagonally into ¾ in/1.5 cm rounds. Arrange the endives on a serving platter. Put the chopped eggs in a bowl.
2. Add the French Dressing to the eggs and toss gently.
3. Add the prosciutto, salt, pepper and parsley to the bowl. Toss.
4. Heap the prosciutto mixture in the center of the endive rounds and serve.

INGREDIENTS/TO SERVE 6

6 heads endive

2 hard-cooked eggs, finely chopped

1 cup French Dressing (see page 34)

¼ lb thinly sliced prosciutto, diced

⅛ teaspoon salt

¼ teaspoon freshly ground black pepper

2 tablespoons fresh parsley, chopped

● *Photograph opposite, below*

Fennel Salad

INGREDIENTS/TO SERVE 4

1 medium fennel

4 radishes, thinly sliced

2 oranges, peeled and sectioned

4 black olives, pitted and halved

4 tablespoons finely chopped onion

several torn feathers from fennel

6 tablespoons olive oil

3 tablespoons cider vinegar

1 teaspoon Pernod or anisette

½ teaspoon salt

⅛ teaspoon cayenne pepper

• Photograph opposite, above

The anise-tasting leaves of the fennel plant lend an interesting tang to a salad, especially when teamed with a Pernod vinaigrette.

1. Slice the bulb and stalks of the fennel into rings. Place in a serving bowl. Arrange the radishes, orange sections, olive, onion, and torn fennel feathers around the fennel.
2. In a mixing bowl whisk together the oil, vinegar, Pernod, salt, and pepper. Pour over the salad and serve.

Wilted Lettuce Salad

INGREDIENTS/TO SERVE 4–6

½ head Boston or romaine lettuce

½ head mignonette lettuce

4 rashers uncooked bacon

2 tablespoons sugar

¼ cup vinegar

4 whole green onions, chopped

¼ teaspoon freshly ground black pepper

• Photograph opposite

For the American pioneers in the nineteenth century, this salad was ideal. It was made from readily available wild salad greens and the omnipresent salt pork. Today, in more settled times, lettuce and bacon have replaced dandelion leaves and salt pork. Serve this salad with simple main courses of roast meat or poultry.

1. Tear the lettuces into large pieces and arrange them artistically in a salad bowl.
2. In a skillet, fry the bacon until crisp. Remove the bacon pieces from the skillet and add them to the salad bowl.
3. Add the sugar and vinegar to the bacon fat remaining in the skillet. Stir until the sugar dissolves.
4. Pour the hot dressing over the salad to 'wilt' the lettuce. Add the green onions and pepper to the bacon. Toss well and serve.

Snow Pea Salad

INGREDIENTS/TO SERVE 4

24 snow peas, fresh or frozen

6 to 8 marinated artichoke hearts, drained and chopped

½ cup bamboo shoots, drained

12 water chestnuts, sliced

¾ cup Chinese cabbage, shredded

8 large mushrooms, thinly sliced

1 cup Chinese Dressing (see page 36)

2 tablespoons chopped fresh parsley

● Photograph opposite

The bright snow pea pods in this salad make a colorful accompaniment to fish and chicken dishes. An equal amount of Touch of Asia Dressing (see page 37) may be substituted for the Chinese Dressing. Bamboo shoots, water chestnuts, Chinese cabbage and snow peas are all staple Asian foods that should be available in oriental food shops.

1. In a pan of lightly salted boiling water, cook the snow peas for 1 minute or until they turn bright green. Drain well. Rinse the snow peas in cold water and drain well again.
2. Put the snow peas, artichoke hearts, bamboo shoots, water chestnuts, Chinese cabbage and mushrooms in a bowl. Toss.
3. Add the Chinese dressing and toss again until well mixed. Garnish with the parsley and serve.

Moroccan Salad

INGREDIENTS/TO SERVE 6

¾ cup olive oil

3 tablespoons red wine vinegar

3 teaspoons ground cumin

1 teaspoon salt

1 teaspoon freshly ground black pepper

3 large sweet green peppers, seeded and diced

3 medium-sized tomatoes, seeded and sliced

1 tablespoon chopped fresh parsley

This is a simplified version of the classic Moroccan Green Pepper Salad (see page 76). It can be made several hours in advance. Serve it after a main course of roast meat, especially lamb. Any leftover salad will still taste good the next evening.

1. Combine the olive oil, vinegar, cumin, salt and pepper in a salad bowl. Stir with a fork until well mixed.
2. Add the green peppers and tomatoes. Toss well. Refrigerate until thoroughly chilled, about 2 to 3 hours. Sprinkle with parsley and toss.

Irvin Cobb's Brown Derby Salad

This is a version of the popular salad served at the Brown Derby restaurant in Hollywood during the 1930s and 1940s. It was invented and consumed in large quantities by the noted American humorist, writer and actor Irvin Cobb. There are many variations on the original recipe, but they all have one thing in common: the ingredients are cut into incredibly tiny pieces. Paprika Dressing (see page 35) may be substituted for the French Dressing. No matter which dressing you use, add it in front of your guests with a flourish, and toss dramatically. Nostalgia reigns supreme with this salad — serve it to your favorite movie stars.

1. On a large serving platter arrange the iceberg lettuce, chicory, endive, romaine lettuce and watercress.
2. Add the remaining ingredients except for the dressing in distinct layers, in any order. Chill for 30 minutes.
3. In front of your guests, add the dressing with a flourish and toss dramatically.

INGREDIENTS/TO SERVE 6–8

½ head iceberg lettuce, torn in pieces

1 head Belgian endive, leaves separated

⅔ bunch chicory, torn in pieces

⅓ head romaine lettuce, torn in pieces

⅔ bunch watercress, torn into sprigs

2 medium-sized tomatoes, finely diced

3 cups boiled chicken, diced

1 sweet green pepper, seeded and finely chopped

1 sweet red pepper, seeded and finely chopped

¼ cup crisply cooked bacon, crumbled into tiny pieces

1 avocado, finely chopped

3 tablespoons finely chopped green onion

3 hard-cooked eggs, finely chopped

¼ cup Romano cheese, grated

1⅓ cups French Dressing (see page 34)

● Photograph opposite

California Salad

In California where tomatoes and oranges grow all year round this salad is very popular. Serve it with steak, or with roast veal or pork.

1. Put the spinach, chicory, Boston and romaine lettuces in a large salad bowl. Chill for 1 hour.
2. When ready to serve, remove the salad from the refrigerator and add the oranges, tomatoes, mushrooms and capers. Toss lightly.
3. Add the honey to the dressing and mix well. Pour the dressing over the salad, toss and serve.

INGREDIENTS/TO SERVE 8

1 lb spinach, stems removed and leaves torn into bite-sized pieces

½ head chicory, torn into bite-sized pieces

1 head Boston lettuce, torn into bite-sized pieces

½ head romaine lettuce, torn into bite-sized pieces

1½ cups mandarin orange slices (if canned, drained)

2 tomatoes, seeded and diced

2 large mushrooms, sliced

2 tablespoons drained capers

2 tablespoons honey

1⅓ cups Paprika Dressing (see page 35)

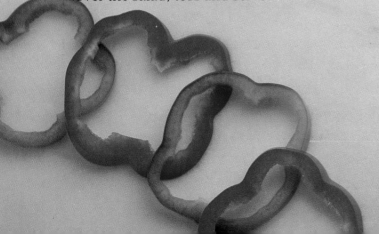

Chinese Pickled Cabbage and Cauliflower

INGREDIENTS/MAKES 8 CUPS

4 cups water

3 tablespoons salt

6 tablespoons sugar

5 tablespoons distilled wine vinegar

½ teaspoon whole peppercorns, Szechuan if possible

¾ teaspoon crushed hot red pepper flakes

4 cups cabbage, coarsely shredded

2 cups cauliflower, in florets

● *Photograph opposite*

This hearty mixture is more of a relish than a true salad. Serve it as a side dish with simple meat dishes, especially with pork and lamb. The leftover salad can be stored in the refrigerator for a week or more.

1. Put the water, salt, sugar and vinegar into a 2-quart wide-mouthed jar. Stir until the sugar and salt are dissolved. Add the peppercorns and red pepper flakes. Stir again.
2. Add the cabbage and cauliflower in layers, pressing each down to the bottom. All of the cabbage and cauliflower should be covered by the water.
3. Cover the jar and let stand for 24 hours at room temperature. Put the jar, still covered, in the refrigerator for 3 to 4 days.
4. Drain the liquid from the jar and serve the cabbage and cauliflower cold. Leftover salad may be stored in the refrigerator for a week or more.

Spinach and Bacon Salad

INGREDIENTS/TO SERVE 8–10

1 lb fresh spinach

2 heads red leaf lettuce

½ lb bacon, fried, drained and crumbled

¼ cup sugar

1 teaspoon salt

1 teaspoon dry mustard

1 tablespoon onion juice

⅓ cup cider vinegar

1 tablespoon poppy seeds

1 cup pure olive oil

1½ cups cottage cheese

This is a substantial salad that can be served with a main course or by itself. Served with some chilled white wine, it makes an elegant lunch. The recipe calls for fresh onion juice. To make this, cut an onion in half horizontally. Scrape the cut surface of the onion with the back of a knife, pulling the knife towards you. The juice will collect against the knife and on the surface of the onion.

1. Remove and discard the tough stems from the spinach. Tear the leaves into large pieces. Tear the lettuce leaves into large pieces. Put the spinach and lettuce in a large salad bowl and add the crumbled bacon.
2. Put the sugar, salt, mustard, onion juice, cider vinegar, poppy seeds, and olive oil into a large jar with a tightly-fitting lid. Cover tightly and shake well.
3. Pour half the dressing on to the salad and toss lightly.
4. Add the cottage cheese to the remaining dressing in the jar and shake until thoroughly mixed.
5. Pour the remaining dressing with the cottage cheese on to the salad. Toss and serve.

Som Tom

This exotic Thai vegetable salad is sweet and hot. If you serve it before the main course, don't serve soup as well. If you serve it after the main course, skip dessert. Dried shrimps and fish sauce are available from oriental supermarkets. Follow the directions on the packet for soaking the shrimps. There is no real substitute but if the sauce is not available, the flavor can be approximated by substituting 1 tablespoon of vinegar mixed with 1 tablespoon of anchovy paste. Do this only as a last resort.

1. Make a bed of pak-choi on a serving platter.
2. Arrange the cucumber strips, cabbage shreds, papaya slices, dried shrimps and tomatoes on the pak-choi.
3. In a jar with a tightly fitting lid combine the fish sauce, brown sugar, green onion and lime or lemon juice. Cover tightly and shake until the sugar dissolves.
4. Add the black pepper, cayenne pepper and garlic and shake again.
5. Pour the dressing over the salad.
6. Sprinkle the peanuts over the salad and serve.

INGREDIENTS/TO SERVE 6

½ head pak-choi or chard

¼ cup cucumber, peeled and cut in strips

¼ cup cabbage, shredded

1 papaya, peeled, seeded and sliced

½ lb dried shrimps, soaked and drained

2 firm tomatoes, quartered

2 tablespoons fish sauce

1½ tablespoons brown sugar

1 tablespoon chopped green onion

3 tablespoons fresh lime juice

2 teaspoons ground black pepper

1½ teaspoons cayenne pepper

2 garlic cloves, finely chopped

2 tablespoons roasted peanuts

GARNISH

Tomato Butterfly garnish (page 23)

● Photograph opposite

Danish Mushroom and Watercress Salad

A good salad for both informal and formal menus — and for experimenting with flavored vinegars. The recipe calls for white wine vinegar, but any sort can be used. Some people prefer a sourer flavor when the salad contains mushrooms.

1. In a blender combine the mustard and 1 tablespoon olive oil. Blend until well mixed.
2. Slowly add the remaining olive oil, a tablespoon at a time, while continuously blending. The mixture should have the look and texture of homemade mayonnaise.
3. Add the vinegar, sugar, shallots, salt, cumin and pepper. Blend until well mixed.
4. Arrange the raddicchio and endive leaves in a salad bowl. Put the mushrooms on top. Pour the dressing over the mushrooms and toss. Refrigerate for 1 hour.
5. Remove the tough stems from the watercress. Remove the salad from the refrigerator and add the watercress. Toss the mushrooms again and serve.

INGREDIENTS/TO SERVE 4–6

1 tablespoon Dijon-style mustard

½ cup pure olive oil

2 tablespoons white wine vinegar

⅛ teaspoon sugar

2 tablespoons finely chopped shallots

¼ teaspoon salt

⅛ teaspoon ground cumin

¼ teaspoon freshly ground black pepper

8–10 leaves radicchio

8–10 leaves endive

¾ lb mushrooms, trimmed and thinly sliced

1 bunch watercress

● Photograph opposite, above

Tarama Salad

INGREDIENTS/TO SERVE 6–8

3 large potatoes

3 tablespoons milk

4 oz red caviar or red lumpfish roe

6 tablespoons water

¼ cup fresh lemon juice

1 small onion, finely chopped

¾ cup pure olive oil

● Photograph opposite

More of a dip than a salad, tarama is Greek in origin. Serve it as an hors-d'oeuvre with wedges of warmed pitta bread and such crudités *as raw cauliflower and broccoli florets, strips of carrot, slivers of cucumber and zucchini, quartered radishes or other crisp raw vegetables of your choice.*

1. Peel the potatoes. Cook them in boiling water until very soft, about 20 minutes.
2. Drain the potatoes and put them in a mixing bowl. By hand or with an electric beater, mash the potatoes, slowly adding the milk, until smooth. Add the caviar and water to the potatoes. Mix well.
3. Add the lemon juice and onion to the mixture and mix briefly.
4. Slowly beat in the olive oil. Continue to beat until a smooth paste is formed.
5. Transfer to a serving bowl. Arrange the *crudités* around the dip and serve.

Nam Prik Pak

INGREDIENTS/TO SERVE 6

3 dried red chili peppers, including seeds, chopped

1½ teaspoons blachen, roasted in foil

6 dried shrimps, pounded and finely chopped

3 garlic cloves, finely chopped

1 teaspoon sugar

2 tablespoons fish sauce

3 tablespoons fresh lime or lemon juice

Nam Prik Pak is a hot sauce usually served with raw vegetables, but it is also served with rice, noodles, fish, meat and, upon occasion, even fruit. When served with raw vegetables, it is an excellent hors-d'oeuvre. The blachen must be cooked before using. Wrap in aluminum foil and bake over a high heat for 1½ minutes. Remove the pan from the heat. When the foil has cooled enough to handle, remove the blachen and continue with the recipe.

In Thailand, Nam Prik Pak is served with raw vegetables, roots, leaves, flowers and a bowl of rice. A refreshingly tart and crisp sliced green mango almost always accompanies Nam Prik Pak. To approach an authentic Nam Prik Pak, serve the sauce with raw vegetables, bamboo shoots, Chinese cabbage, mustard greens and perhaps a thinly sliced mango or green apple. Every Thai cook makes a unique version of Nam Prik Pak; by all means, experiment with your own recipe.

1. Put the chili peppers in a blender and blend for 5 seconds. Add the *blachen*, shrimp, garlic and sugar. Blend. Add the fish sauce and lime juice. Blend until well mixed.
2. Pour the Nam Prik Pak into a serving bowl. Serve with a colorful array of chilled raw vegetables.

Avocado and Grapefruit Salad

This salad is ideal served outdoors with barbecued beef, but it is good indoors at any informal dinner.

1. Peel the avocado and cut it into slices. Put the slices in a bowl and sprinkle with the lemon juice.
2. Tear the lettuce into bite-sized pieces. Put the lettuce in a salad bowl.
3. Add the grapefruit, avocado and onion to the salad bowl. Pour over the French dressing. Refrigerate for 30 minutes before serving.

INGREDIENTS/TO SERVE 6

1 ripe avocado

2 tablespoons fresh lemon juice

1 head cos lettuce

1½ cups seeded grapefruit, segments

1 red onion, thinly sliced

1 cup French Dressing (see page 34)

● *Photograph opposite*

Barbecue Salad

The roasted peppers give this salad a barbecue flavor. It is designed to be cooked and served outdoors, but the skewered vegetables can be broiled indoors as well. For an interesting variation, you could substitute 1 cup Touch of Asia Dressing (see page 37) for the Herb Dressing.

1. Thread the tomato, green pepper, red pepper and eggplant quarters and the onion halves on to 6 (or more) long skewers.
2. Lay the skewers on the barbecue grill over white coals or place them under a broiler at a high heat. Cook for 12 to 15 minutes, turning frequently.
3. Remove the skewers from the grill. Remove the vegetables from the skewers. Put the eggplant and tomato pieces in a bowl.
4. While still hot, peel the skin from the pepper pieces. Add the pieces to the salad bowl.
5. Coarsely chop the onions and add them to the salad bowl. Add the Herb Dressing and toss. Refrigerate for 30 minutes before serving.

INGREDIENTS/TO SERVE 4

3 large tomatoes, quartered

2 large sweet green peppers, seeded and quartered

1 sweet red pepper, seeded and quartered

1 large eggplant, peeled and quartered

2 large onions, halved

1 cup Herb Dressing (see page 40)

Japanese Cucumber Salad

INGREDIENTS/TO SERVE 4

2 medium-sized cucumbers, thinly sliced

1 teaspoon salt

¼ cup rice wine vinegar

2 tablespoons soy sauce

1 teaspoon sugar

2 teaspoons white sesame seeds

GARNISH

Cucumber Cone garnish (see page 25)

• Photograph opposite

This Asian salad is an excellent accompaniment to nouvelle cuisine main courses. Some Japanese prefer a very tart taste in this salad and use 3 tablespoons distilled white vinegar instead of ¼ cup rice wine vinegar.

1. Put the cucumber slices in a colander. Sprinkle with the salt. Let the cucumber slices drain for 30 minutes.
2. Remove the cucumber slices from the colander. Put the slices between two layers of paper towels and pat them dry.
3. Into a jar with a tightly fitting lid, put the vinegar, soy sauce and sugar. Cover tightly and shake well until the sugar dissolves.
4. Put the cucumber slices in a salad bowl. Add the dressing and toss lightly.
5. Toast the sesame seeds in a dry skillet over a high heat, shaking the pan frequently. When the seeds begin to jump, remove them from the pan and crush them with a pestle. Sprinkle the crushed sesame seeds on the salad and serve.

Middle Eastern Cole-slaw

INGREDIENTS/TO SERVE 4-6

3 cups cabbage, coarsely shredded

2 to 3 tablespoons salt

1 cup fresh orange juice

3 tablespoons fresh lemon juice

¼ teaspoon sugar

½ teaspoon honey

1 teaspoon hot red pepper flakes

2 teaspoons white wine vinegar

½ teaspoon salt

This Middle Eastern version of cole-slaw is a far cry from the usual bland stuff served with a watery mayonnaise dressing. It keeps its freshness on even the hottest days. Serve it with meat main courses, especially those that are barbecued or broiled.

1. Put the shredded cabbage in a colander. Sprinkle the 2 to 3 tablespoons of salt over the cabbage and let stand for 1 hour.
2. Rinse the salt from the cabbage. Drain. Wrap the cabbage in a kitchen towel and squeeze as much liquid from it as possible.
3. Put the orange juice, lemon juice, sugar, honey, hot red pepper flakes, vinegar and salt in a salad bowl. Stir until mixed. Add the cabbage to the salad bowl and toss well.

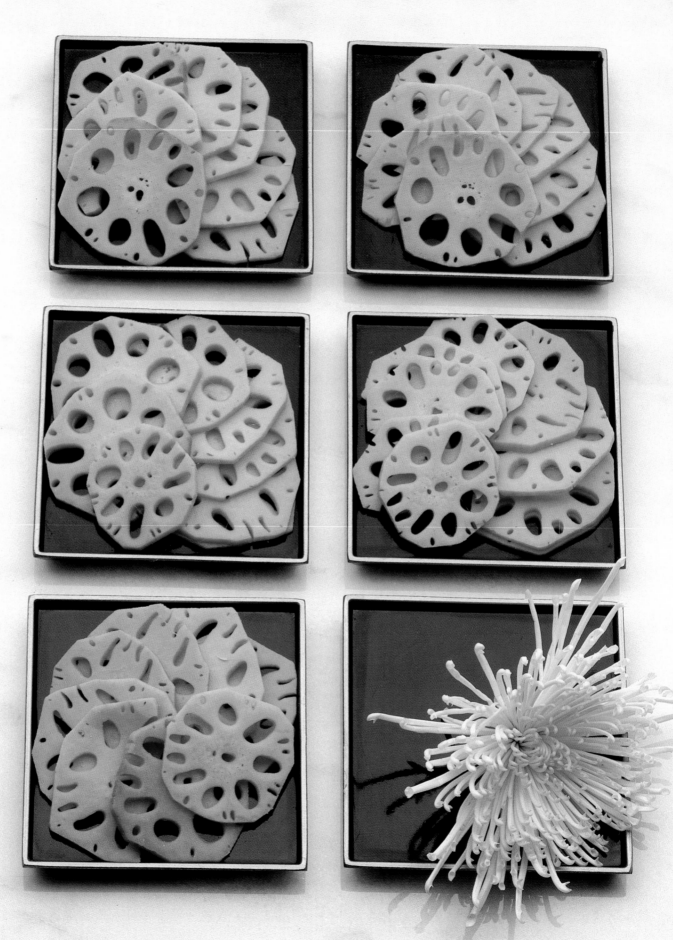

Chinese Lotus Root Salad

INGREDIENTS/TO SERVE 4–6

1 lb fresh (or canned) lotus roots, carefully washed and peeled

4 cups boiling water

1 tablespoon soy sauce

2 tablespoons white wine vinegar

1 tablespoon sugar

1 tablespoon peanut oil

2 tablespoons sesame oil

¼ teaspoon salt

● *Photograph opposite*

Lotus root is found fresh, canned or dried in oriental food shops. If possible, use fresh lotus root for this salad. The canned and dried versions have different textures and tastes. This is a delicate salad that goes best with nouvelle cuisine *main courses.*

1. Cut off and discard the ends of the lotus roots. With a very sharp knife, cut the lotus roots into ⅛ in (3mm) rounds. To prevent discoloration, drop the slices as they are cut into a large bowl with enough cold water to cover.
2. Drain the lotus root slices and add the boiling water. Soak for 5 minutes. Drain and rinse with cold water. Drain again. Using paper towels, pat the lotus root slices completely dry.
3. Into a jar with a tightly fitting lid put the soy sauce, vinegar, sugar, peanut oil, sesame oil and salt. Cover tightly and shake until the sugar and salt are dissolved.
4. Arrange the lotus root slices in overlapping concentric circles on serving plates.
5. Pour the dressing over the lotus root slices. Chill for 1½ hours before serving.

Swedish Tomato Salad

INGREDIENTS/TO SERVE 6

6 large tomatoes, seeded and halved

¾ cup walnut oil

⅓ cup white wine vinegar

2 garlic cloves, crushed

¾ teaspoon dried dill

¼ teaspoon sugar

¼ teaspoon honey

½ teaspoon Dijon-style mustard

2 tablespoons chopped fresh chives

½ teaspoon salt

¼ teaspoon freshly ground black pepper

6 to 8 lettuce leaves

6 fresh parsley sprigs

Fresh, garden-ripened tomatoes are important for this recipe. If only shop-bought tomatoes are available, marinate them for an hour longer (3½ instead of 2½ hours). This should soften the hardest tomatoes and give flavor to the blandest. Serve this salad as a first course or as an accompaniment to simple fish, veal or poultry dishes.

1. Put the tomatoes, cut-side down, in a shallow dish.
2. Put the walnut oil, vinegar, garlic, dill, sugar, honey, mustard, chives, salt and pepper in a jar with a tightly fitting lid. Cover tightly and shake vigorously until all the ingredients are blended.
3. Pour the dressing over the tomatoes. Chill the salad for 2½ hours. Every 30 minutes spoon the dressing over the tomatoes.
4. Line a serving dish with lettuce leaves. Remove the tomatoes from the dish and place them on the lettuce leaves. Pour the dressing over the tomatoes. Garnish with the parsley sprigs and serve.

German Potato Salad

The dill in this recipe is what makes it German. Serve it with fried chicken, cold roast beef or ham. Store potatoes in a cool, dark place, but do not refrigerate them. Cold temperatures speed the conversion of starch in the potato to sugar, resulting in an unpleasant sweet taste.

1. Cook the potatoes, in their skins, in a large pot of lightly salted boiling water. Drain well, peel while warm and dice. (Leave small potatoes whole and unpeeled, if you prefer.)
2. Put the potatoes in a salad bowl and add the green onions. garlic, capers, dill and parsley. Toss lightly.
3. Into a jar with a tightly fitting lid, put the salt, pepper, olive oil, vinegar, beef stock and sugar. Cover and shake until blended.
4. Pour the dressing over the potato salad and toss lightly. Let stand at room temperature for 1½ hours before serving.

INGREDIENTS/TO SERVE 6

6 large potatoes or 2 lb small potatoes

4 whole green onions finely chopped

1 garlic clove, finely chopped

1 teaspoon drained capers

2 tablespoons chopped fresh dill

2 tablespoons chopped fresh parsley

1 teaspoon salt

1 teaspoon freshly ground black pepper

5 tablespoons pure olive oil

3 tablespoons wine vinegar

1 tablespoon beef stock (optional)

½ teaspoon sugar

● *Photograph opposite*

Traditional Potato Salad

Today, potato salad is usually made with mayonnaise, but at the turn of the century, boiled dressing was the order of the day. This recipe tries to capture some of the boiled dressing flavor in a more convenient mayonnaise dressing. As alternatives, try substituting an equal amount of Sour Cream Dressing (see page 37), Yogurt Mayonnaise (see page 39) or Tofu Mayonnaise (see page 39). All-Purpose Dressing (see page 40) is a less creamy but still very tasty alternative.

1. In a salad bowl, put the potatoes, onion, olives, celery and eggs. Mix lightly.
2. Add the mayonnaise, vinegar, salt and pepper. Toss to coat all the ingredients. Garnish with parsley and serve.

INGREDIENTS/TO SERVE 4–6

7 medium-sized potatoes, peeled, cooked and diced

1 medium-sized onion, finely chopped

2 tablespoons finely chopped pimento-stuffed green olives

½ cup celery, sliced

2 hard-cooked eggs, chopped

¾ cup mayonnaise

2 tablespoons wine vinegar

½ teaspoon salt

1 teaspoon finely ground black pepper

2 tablespoons chopped fresh parsley

Tomato and Mozzarella Salad

INGREDIENTS/TO SERVE 4

2 to 3 large tomatoes, thinly sliced

4 oz fresh Mozzarella cheese, thinly sliced

2 tablespoons fresh basil

⅓ cup extra virgin olive oil

¼ teaspoon salt

½ teaspoon freshly ground black pepper

• Photograph opposite

No lemon juice or vinegar is needed with the oil for this wonderful first-course salad. The natural acidity of the tomatoes will do nicely. The fresher the tomatoes the better the salad.

1. Arrange the tomatoes and Mozzarella in alternating layers in a serving dish.
2. Garnish the salad with the basil.
3. Sprinkle the salad with the olive oil and with the salt and pepper. Serve.

Italian Zucchini Salad

INGREDIENTS/TO SERVE 4

2 medium-sized zucchini

½ cup pure olive oil

3 tablespoons red wine vinegar

1 green onion, white part only, finely chopped

½ teaspoon dried basil

⅛ teaspoon dried oregano

⅛ teaspoon dried marjoram

1 garlic clove, crushed

¼ teaspoon salt

2 tablespoons chopped fresh parsley

½ teaspoon freshly ground black pepper

Also known as courgettes, vegetable marrow, Italian squash and cocozelle, zucchini are popular vegetables, especially in Italy, France and Greece. This salad is a good accompaniment to pasta or fish dishes.

1. Cook the zucchini in a pot of salted boiling water for 7 to 8 minutes. Drain well and rinse in very cold water for 5 minutes. Drain well again. Slice the zucchini very thinly.
2. Put the olive oil, vinegar, green onion, basil, oregano, marjoram, garlic and salt in a jar with a tightly fitting lid. Cover tightly and shake until well blended.
3. Put the zucchini and the dressing in a salad bowl. Toss very gently. Let stand for 15 to 20 minutes. Sprinkle with parsley and pepper and serve.

Cachcombar

Serve this Indian tomato and onion salad for a refreshing end to a rich meal. The salad contains a lot of onion, so garnish each plate with a few fresh parsley sprigs. Parsley is a very effective natural breath freshener.

1. Put the ginger, coriander, lime juice, salt and pepper in a jar with a tightly fitting lid. Cover tightly and shake until the salt dissolves.
2. Arrange the tomatoes and onions on a serving dish. Sprinkle with the green and chili peppers.
3. Pour the lime juice dressing over the salad. Let the salad stand at room temperature for 30 minutes before serving.

INGREDIENTS/TO SERVE 4

1 teaspoon finely chopped fresh ginger

1 tablespoon chopped fresh coriander or parsley

4 tablespoons fresh lime juice

¼ teaspoon salt

¼ teaspoon freshly ground black pepper

3 large tomatoes, seeded and sliced

2 medium-sized white onions, sliced into rings

¼ cup sweet green pepper, chopped

2 hot green chili peppers, seeded and coarsely chopped

● Photograph opposite, above

Moroccan Green Pepper Salad

This salad is a favorite in Morocco. For a more authentic flavor, use two seeded, chopped chili peppers instead of the crushed hot red pepper flakes. Serve this salad as a flavorful accompaniment to meat stews and couscous.

1. Preheat the broiler. Put the peppers and tomatoes on a baking sheet and cook, turning occasionally, until the skins blister.
2. Remove the vegetables from the heat. When they are cool enough to handle, remove the skins and seeds from the peppers and tomatoes.
3. Chop the peppers, tomatoes and onions. Put them in a salad bowl.
4. Put the olive oil, lemon juice, cumin, red pepper flakes and coriander in a jar with a tightly fitting lid. Cover tightly and shake well.
5. Pour the dressing over the salad and toss. Marinate in the refrigerator for 1½ hours, tossing occasionally.
6. Remove the salad from the refrigerator. Garnish with the olives and anchovies.

INGREDIENTS/TO SERVE 6

6 large sweet green peppers

6 large tomatoes

2 medium-sized onions

⅓ cup pure olive oil

3 tablespoons fresh lemon juice

1 tablespoon ground cumin

¼ teaspoon crushed hot red pepper flakes

¾ teaspoon chopped fresh coriander

6 black olives

6 anchovy fillets

● Photograph opposite, below

Russian Radish and Cucumber Zakusky

Zakusky is the Russian word for appetizer or starter. A zakusky appears well before the main course, always accompanied by ice-cold vodka that is served in small glasses and drunk in one gulp. In the old days of imperial Russia, the custom was to start washing down the zakusky with vodka several hours before the lavish dinner began. Now zakusky is no longer the appetizer of nobility.

1. Remove the yolks from the eggs. Put them in a small mixing bowl and mash well with a fork. Chop the whites and set them aside.
2. Add the sour cream, salt, pepper and 2 tablespoons of the dill to the mixing bowl. Stir until well blended.
3. Arrange the radishes and cucumber slices on a serving platter.
4. Add the egg yolk and sour cream mixture. Garnish with the remaining dill and the chopped egg whites, and serve with black bread.

INGREDIENTS/TO SERVE 4–6

2 hard-cooked eggs

1 cup sour cream

¾ teaspoon salt

1 teaspoon freshly ground black pepper

3 tablespoons chopped fresh dill

1 cup radishes, thinly sliced

1 large cucumber, peeled, seeded and thinly sliced

● *Photograph opposite, above*

Thai Water Chestnut Salad

Water chestnuts, often thought to be found only in China, in fact grow throughout Asia, Europe and North America. Canned water chestnuts are easily found in grocery stores and oriental supermarkets. This salad makes an excellent light meal on its own. The crisp texture of the water chestnut makes it a good accompaniment to simple fish and poultry dishes.

1. Heat the peanut oil in a skillet. Add the garlic and onion and sauté until golden brown. Put the garlic, onion and oil in a large mixing bowl.
2. Add the fish sauce, brown sugar and lime juice to the mixing bowl. Stir until the sugar dissolves. Add the pork, mint and coriander. Toss gently.
3. Arrange the mixture on a platter with the water chestnuts and shrimp around the pork mixture. Garnish with strips of red chili pepper and serve.

INGREDIENTS/TO SERVE 6

2 tablespoons peanut oil

4 garlic cloves, finely chopped

1 medium-sized white onion, finely chopped

2 tablespoons fish sauce

1 tablespoon brown sugar

⅓ cup fresh lime juice

½ cup cooked ground pork

1 tablespoon chopped fresh mint leaves

3 tablespoons chopped coriander

2 cups water chestnuts, drained

6 cooked shrimp, shelled and chopped

2 red chili peppers, seeded and cut diagonally into strips.

● *Photograph opposite, below*

Bean and Tuna Salad

INGREDIENTS/TO SERVE 6

2 cups cooked cannellini or other white beans, drained

½ cup extra virgin olive oil

3 tablespoons fresh lemon juice

1 teaspoon salt

½ teaspoon freshly ground black pepper

1 onion, thinly sliced

8 black olives, pitted and halved

6 to 8 oz canned tuna, drained

2 tablespoons chopped fresh parsley

2 tablespoons chopped fresh basil

● Photograph opposite, above

The Tuscan dish was originally called fagioli freschi al tonno, *and was served as a hot main course, but some time in the culinary past it became a cold antipasto. Any sort of white bean may be used instead of cannellini beans, for example haricot beans.*

1. Put the beans into a large salad bowl.
2. Put the olive oil, lemon juice, salt and pepper in a jar with a tightly fitting lid. Cover tightly and shake well. Pour the dressing over the beans.
3. Add the onion slices and black olives to the salad and toss. Add the tuna and toss again. Sprinkle the parsley and basil over the salad. Serve.

Chick Pea Salad

INGREDIENTS/TO SERVE 6

¼ cup raisins

2½ cups cooked chick peas

½ cup sweet red pepper, diced

½ cup green onions, white parts only, finely chopped

2 tablespoons chopped pimento

3 tablespoons chopped fresh parsley

⅓ cup pure olive oil

3 tablespoons fresh lemon juice

½ teaspoon dried thyme

¼ teaspoon salt

½ teaspoon freshly ground black pepper

3 tablespoons chopped pimento-stuffed green olives

● Photograph opposite, below

Chick peas are particularly popular in southern Europe. They were one of the first foods introduced to the New World by the Spanish explorers. This salad goes well with main courses of lamb or pork. Soak dried chick peas overnight, then boil for 2 to 3 hours, or use ready-cooked, canned chick peas.

1. Put the raisins in a small bowl and add enough cold water to cover. Soak the raisins for 30 minutes. Drain well.
2. Combine the chick peas, red pepper, raisins, green onion, pimento and parsley in a salad bowl. Toss.
3. Put the olive oil, lemon juice, thyme, salt and pepper in a jar with a tightly fitting lid. Cover tightly and shake until the salt dissolves. Pour the dressing over the salad and toss well. Chill for 1½ hours.
4. Remove the salad from the refrigerator. Toss, garnish with chopped olives, and serve.

Italian Fontina Cheese Salad

Produced in northern Italy, Fontina is a velvety-textured, mild-tasting cheese that combines well with other ingredients. Serve this salad with a dry red wine for an elegant first course.

1. Preheat the broiler.
2. Place the yellow and red peppers on a baking sheet and broil until the skins are blistered and slightly blackened, about 10 to 15 minutes. Remove the peppers from the heat.
3. When the peppers are cool enough to handle, remove the blistered skin. Cut the peppers into strips about ⅜ in (9 mm) wide. Put the pepper strips, Fontina cheese and olives in a serving bowl.
4. Put the olive oil, mustard, cream, green onion, salt and pepper in a jar with a tightly fitting lid. Cover tightly and shake until well blended.
5. Pour the dressing over the salad and toss. Chill the salad for 1 to 2 hours. Garnish with the chopped parsley and toss again lightly before serving.

INGREDIENTS/TO SERVE 6

2 large sweet yellow peppers, seeded and halved

2 large sweet red peppers, seeded and halved

½ lb Fontina cheese, diced

¼ cup pitted green olives, thinly sliced

⅓ cup pure olive oil

1½ teaspoons Dijon-style mustard

3 tablespoons cream

1 tablespoon chopped green onion

¾ teaspoon salt

1 teaspoon freshly ground black pepper

1 tablespoon chopped fresh parsley

● *Photograph opposite*

Lentil and Feta Cheese Salad

Feta is a crumbly cheese that is very common in Greece and the Middle East. It is readily available from cheese shops and supermarkets. Serve this salad with fish and chicken dishes.

1. Put the lentils in a bowl. Add 2½ cups cold water and soak the lentils for 2 hours. Drain.
2. Put the lentils in a saucepan and add enough cold water to cover them completely. Add the bay leaf, basil and 1 garlic clove. Bring to the boil and simmer, covered, for 20 minutes.
3. Add the celery and onion. Add enough additional water to cover the lentils. Cover the saucepan and simmer for 10 more minutes.
4. Drain the lentils, celery and onion and discard the bay leaf and garlic clove.
5. Put the lentils, celery and onion in a serving bowl. Add the chives and feta cheese. Toss.
6. Put the olive oil, vinegar, oregano, remaining garlic clove, salt and pepper in a jar with a tightly fitting lid. Cover tightly and shake until well blended.
7. Pour the dressing over the lentil salad and toss. Let the salad stand for 2 hours, tossing occasionally, before serving.

INGREDIENTS/TO SERVE 6

1½ cups brown lentils

1 bay leaf

½ teaspoon dried basil

2 garlic cloves, crushed

½ cup celery, diced

1 small onion, chopped

½ cup fresh chives, chopped

¾ cup feta cheese, crumbled

6 tablespoons virgin olive oil

3 tablespoons wine vinegar

⅛ teaspoon dried oregano

½ teaspoon salt

½ teaspoon freshly ground black pepper

● *Photograph opposite*

Nepalese Egg Salad

Visually, this salad looks like the snow-covered foothills of the Himalayas, shrouded in a low-hanging mist. It tastes just as exotic. Serve it as a cooling accompaniment to curry or any spicy dish.

1. Melt the butter in a small skillet. Add the chili pepper, cumin and cardamom. Carefully sauté the mixture, being careful not to burn it. This will fix the mixed spice flavor and rid the spices of their 'raw' taste. Remove the skillet from the heat. Drain the spices on paper towels and set aside.
2. Into a mixing bowl, put the yogurt, coriander, lime and salt. Stir briefly. Add the reserved spices and mix well.
3. Arrange the eggs on a serving dish then pour the dressing over the eggs.

INGREDIENTS/TO SERVE 6

1½ tablespoons butter

2 teaspoons chopped chili pepper

1 teaspoon ground cumin

¼ teaspoon ground cardamom

1½ cups unflavored yogurt

5 tablespoons chopped fresh coriander

1 small lime with peel, finely chopped

¼ teaspoon salt

6–8 hard-cooked eggs, halved

● Photograph opposite

Traditional Egg Salad

Anchovies are not strictly traditional in egg salad, but they do add a lot of flavor and the needed saltiness. Egg salad goes well with cold meat or fried chicken, especially when served at picnics and buffets. Of course, it's delicious in sandwiches as well.

1. Put the egg, celery, anchovies and green onion in a mixing bowl. Toss gently.
2. Add the mayonnaise, cayenne pepper, salt and pepper. Toss until all the ingredients are coated. Chill for 1 to 2 hours.
3. Line 4 individual salad plates with the lettuce leaves. Remove the egg salad from the refrigerator and spoon it on to each plate evenly. Garnish each plate with a tomato quarter and serve.

INGREDIENTS/TO SERVE 4

6 hard-cooked eggs, chopped

½ cup celery, chopped

5 anchovy fillets, chopped

3 tablespoons chopped green onion

½ cup mayonnaise

⅛ teaspoon cayenne pepper

½ teaspoon salt

½ teaspoon freshly ground black pepper

4 to 8 lettuce leaves

1 large tomato, quartered

Salmon Salad

INGREDIENTS/SERVES 4

6 tablespoons raspberry vinegar

3 tablespoons finely chopped shallots

¾ cup pure olive oil

½ teaspoon salt

freshly ground black pepper to taste

¼ cup clarified butter

½ lb thickly sliced salmon fillet

2 small heads iceberg or Boston lettuce

½ cucumber, finely sliced

GARNISH

Cucumber cone garnish (see page 25)

● Photograph opposite

Serve this creation of the nouvelle cuisine *as a main course. Any fruit vinegar, not just raspberry, may be used. Be sure to sauté the salmon as briefly as possible so that it doesn't dry out.*

1. In a small mixing bowl, combine the vinegar and shallots. In a slow, steady stream, whisk in the olive oil. Continue to whisk until well blended. Add the salt and pepper and whisk again. Set aside.
2. In a large skillet, melt the butter over a high heat. Add the salmon and sauté briefly for 1 to 2 minutes. Remove the pan from the heat.
3. Arrange the lettuce leaves on a large serving platter. Arrange the salmon slices on the lettuce.
4. Whisk the dressing again and pour it evenly over the salmon. Serve warm, garnished with the sliced cucumber.

Scallops Seviche

INGREDIENTS/TO SERVE 6

1 cup fresh lemon juice

1 cup fresh lime juice

3 tablespoons crushed hot red pepper flakes

1 large garlic clove, finely chopped

2 lb raw scallops, coarsely chopped

2 large tomatoes, seeded and chopped

1 avocado, peeled and diced

¼ cup green onion, finely chopped

½ teaspoon salt

½ teaspoon freshly ground black pepper

1 head romaine lettuce torn into bite-sized pieces

The ancient Incas in Peru made the first seviche. Marinating seafood in lemon and lime juice was an easy meal since it required no cooking. This recipe calls for fresh scallops, but any firm, white-fleshed fish such as cod or halibut cut into small pieces could be used instead. Serve seviche as a first course or luncheon main course with a dry white wine.

1. Put the lemon and lime juice in a large mixing bowl. Add the red pepper and garlic. Stir.
2. Add the scallops. If there is not enough of the lemon/lime juice to cover the scallops, add more until they are covered. Stir well. Refrigerate for 3 hours. The scallops will turn white from blanching in the marinade.
3. Put the tomatoes, avocado, green onion, salt and pepper into a large mixing bowl. Toss.
4. Drain the scallops, reserving ¼ cup of the marinade. Add the scallops to the tomato and avocado mixture. Add the reserved marinade to the salad and toss. Let stand at room temperature for 30 minutes, tossing occasionally.
5. Make a bed of the romaine lettuce on a serving platter. Drain the salad and arrange it on the lettuce. Serve.

Greek Swordfish Salad

Any firm-fleshed fish, such as halibut or salmon, may be used in this recipe. This is an excellent main course in warm weather.

1. Put the swordfish steaks in a single layer in a large skillet. Add the water, marjoram, bay leaf, peppercorns, onion, olive oil, lemon slices and salt. Cover the pan and simmer over a medium heat until the swordfish flakes easily, about 8 to 9 minutes.
2. After it has cooled, remove the swordfish from the pan. Put the steaks on a plate, cover, and refrigerate for 1½ hours.
3. Strain the liquid from the skillet into a medium-sized saucepan. Cook the fish stock over moderate heat until it is reduced to about ½ cup.
4. In a mixing bowl beat the egg yolks, cayenne pepper and lemon juice until well blended. Add the fish stock, still warm, to the egg-yolk mixture. Beat until well blended.
5. Put the fish stock mixture into the top of a double boiler. Cook over boiling water, stirring constantly, until the dressing thickens. Remove the top half of the boiler and let cool.
6. Slowly add the sour cream, stirring continuously until well blended. Pour into a bowl, cover and refrigerate for 1 hour.
7. Line a large serving platter with lettuce leaves. Put the swordfish steaks on the lettuce and arrange the tomato slices around the fish. Spoon the dressing onto the fish. Sprinkle the salad with shrimp. Garnish with black olives and serve.

INGREDIENTS/TO SERVE 6

2 lb swordfish steaks
1½ cups water
½ teaspoon dried marjoram
1 bay leaf
5 whole black peppercorns
1 small onion, quartered
1 tablespoon pure olive oil
4 lemon slices
½ teaspoon salt
2 egg yolks
⅛ teaspoon cayenne pepper
1 tablespoon fresh lemon juice
½ cup sour cream
1 head romaine lettuce
2 medium-sized tomatoes, thinly sliced
1 cup cooked shrimp, coarsely chopped
12 black olives

Smoked White Fish Salad

The vodka in this recipe gives it its Russian accent — never omit it. Smoked Fish Salad is a perfect way to start a weekend brunch; it is also good as a starter for any lunch or dinner.

1. With a fork, break the fish into large meaty chunks. Arrange the pieces on serving plates.
2. Mix the sour cream, onion and dill together in a serving bowl.
3. Garnish the dressing with a little more dill and add the vodka. Garnish the fish with watercress and serve.

INGREDIENTS/TO SERVE 6

3 large smoked fish (trout, mackerel, haddock), cleaned and sliced open
1½ cups sour cream
1 large red onion, chopped
1 tablespoon chopped fresh dill or 1 teaspoon dried dill
1 tablespoon vodka
salt to taste
freshly ground black pepper to taste
1 cup watercress, chopped

● *Photograph opposite*

Salade Niçoise

Every chef has his or her own version of this classic salad from the south of France — there is no one true recipe. Some variations substitute cooked mussels for the tuna, add 8 oz of potato salad in vinaigrette dressing, or 8 oz of cooked green (French) beans. Serve this hearty country salad with crusty bread and red wine.

1. Line a salad bowl with the lettuce leaves. Put the tuna, broken into chunks, into the center of the salad bowl. Arrange the anchovies, chopped egg, pepper strips, tomato wedges and black olives in circles radiating out from the center. The salad should look like a multicolored wheel attached to a tuna fish.
2. Sprinkle the onion rings, parsley and chopped green olives over the salad.
3. Pour the dressing over the salad at the table just before serving. Do not toss!

INGREDIENTS/TO SERVE 4–6

1 head Boston lettuce or garden lettuce

14 oz tuna, drained

6 anchovy fillets

2 hard-cooked eggs, chopped

2 green peppers, seeded and cut into strips

3 large tomatoes, cut into wedges

12 black olives, pitted

½ small Bermuda onion, sliced into rings

1 tablespoon chopped fresh parsley

1 tablespoon chopped, pitted green olives

¾ cup French Dressing (see page 34)

● Photograph opposite

Tofu and Tuna Salad

Quick, easy, nutritious and cheap, this salad was invented by a friend studying in Asia. Serve it as a starter or at lunch. Shallots may be substituted for the onions.

1. Put the tuna, tofu, onion, green onion and pepper in a bowl. With a wooden spoon stir until blended. Add the mayonnaise and stir again.
2. Serve.

INGREDIENTS/TO SERVE 4

6 oz tuna, drained

1 cake tofu (bean curd)

2 tablespoons chopped onion

4 green onions, finely chopped

1 medium-sized green pepper, coarsely chopped

¼ cup mayonnaise

½ teaspoon salt

Italian Seafood Salad

INGREDIENTS/TO SERVE 6

1 lb cooked mussels

1 lb cooked clams

1 lb cooked cockles

1 lb cooked shrimps

1 lb cooked jumbo shrimp

1 lb baby octopus in oil

¾ cup extra virgin olive oil

3 tablespoons fresh lemon juice

1 teaspoon Dijon-style mustard

1 tablespoon chopped fresh parsley

1 tablespoon chopped fresh basil or 1 teaspoon dried

½ teaspoon freshly ground black pepper

● Photograph opposite

This grand seafood salad is superb as a main course at lunch or dinner. The proportions of the various ingredients may be varied to suit availability and taste.

1. Arrange the different seafood on a large serving platter, in whatever arrangement pleases you.
2. Put the olive oil, lemon juice, mustard, parsley, basil and pepper in a jar with a tightly fitting lid. Cover tightly and shake well. Let stand for a few minutes.
3. Serve the dressing with the seafood.

Crabmeat Salad with Hot Caper Dressing

INGREDIENTS/TO SERVE 4

5 cups romaine lettuce, torn into bite-sized pieces

1 cup cooked crab meat, still warm

½ cup olive oil

3 tablespoons red wine vinegar

3 tablespoons drained capers

1 garlic clove, finely chopped

¼ teaspoon salt

½ teaspoon dried oregano

freshly ground black pepper to taste

The caper dressing in this recipe will work equally well over cooked lobster meat. Serve the salad with a dry white wine for brunch or as a first course at dinner.

1. Put the romaine lettuce and the crab meat in a salad bowl. Set aside. In a saucepan combine the olive oil, vinegar, capers, garlic, salt, oregano and pepper. Heat just to boiling point. Remove from the heat. Pour the dressing over the lettuce and crab meat. Toss well and serve at once.

Russian Herring Salad

INGREDIENTS/TO SERVE 4

2 cups pickled herring, diced, a few pieces reserved

3 medium-sized potatoes, peeled, boiled and diced

½ cup carrots, diced

1 medium-sized onion, chopped

½ cup sweet gherkin pickles, finely chopped

4 hard-cooked eggs, 2 chopped, 2 quartered

1 cup sour cream

1 tablespoon wine vinegar

2 tablespoons hot prepared mustard

1 teaspoon sugar

1 cup cooked beets, sliced

3 tablespoons chopped fresh dill

2 hard-cooked eggs, quartered

● Photograph opposite

Ideally, this salad is made with Baltic Sea herring pickled in the Russian style. Serve it with ice-cold vodka as an hors-d'oeuvre. It also makes a good main course for lunch or supper.

1. Put the diced herring, potatoes, carrots, onion, gherkins and chopped eggs in a large mixing bowl. Toss until mixed.
2. Put the sour cream, vinegar, mustard and sugar in a small mixing bowl. Stir with a wooden spoon until well blended.
3. Add the sour cream mixture to the salad and toss until the ingredients are coated. Spoon the salad into a serving dish. Arrange the reserved herring pieces and sliced beets on top. Cover and chill for 1 hour.
4. Garnish with the dill and the quartered eggs and serve.

Scandinavian Herring Salad

INGREDIENTS/TO SERVE 4-6

2 salt herrings

2 small apples, cored, and cut into small pieces

2 cups cooked beets, finely chopped

½ cup onion, minced

¼ cup dill pickle, chopped

olive oil

cider vinegar

2 hard-cooked eggs, chopped

lettuce leaves

1. Place the salt herrings in a bowl of cold water to cover. Soak for 2 hours. Drain and carefully flake the meat.
2. Place the herring meat in a mixing bowl. Add the apples, beets, onions and pickle.
3. Dress with oil and vinegar to taste.
4. Toss well. Chill for 2 hours.
5. Remove salad from refrigerator 45 minutes before serving. Toss again, sprinkle with chopped eggs, and serve on lettuce leaves.

Andalusian Mussel Salad

Canned mussels may be used in this recipe, but fresh mussels are infinitely preferable. Serve the salad as a main course for lunch or as a first course.

1. In a small bowl, mash the egg yolk with 2 tablespoons of the olive oil and the garlic. Add the remaining olive oil and the vinegar. Stir well. Add the parsley, salt and pepper. Stir until well blended.
2. In a serving bowl, put the green and red peppers, mussels and chopped green olives. Toss gently. Pour the egg dressing over the salad and toss gently again. Cover the bowl and refrigerate for 30 minutes.
3. Remove the salad from the refrigerator, garnish with the onion rings and black olives and serve.

INGREDIENTS/TO SERVE 4

1 hard-cooked egg yolk

¼ cup pure olive oil

1 garlic clove, finely chopped

4 tablespoons white wine vinegar

1 tablespoon chopped fresh parsley

½ teaspoon salt

½ teaspoon freshly ground black pepper

½ cup green pepper, chopped

½ cup sweet red pepper, chopped

1½ cups fresh mussels, cooked and well drained

6 coarsely chopped pimento-stuffed green olives

1 medium-sized onion, sliced in rings

6 black olives

● *Photograph opposite*

Avocado and Shrimp Salad

This recipe is easily halved to serve two or three. If you do this, leave the stone of the avocado in the unused half; this will keep the avocado from discoloring. For a light lunch or delicious first course, serve the salad with a good white Bordeaux.

1. Put the olive oil, vinegar, green onion, oregano and Tabasco sauce in a jar with tightly fitting lid. Cover tightly and shake until well mixed.
2. Put the shrimp in a mixing bowl. Pour the dressing over the shrimp. Toss lightly and cover. Let marinate for 1 to 2 hours at room temperature.
3. Add the tomato, cucumber, olives, salt, pimento and pepper to the shrimp. Toss lightly.
4. Halve the avocados and remove the stones. Sprinkle the lemon juice on the avocados to retard discoloration.
5. Line a serving platter with lettuce leaves and place the avocado halves on top. Spoon the shrimp salad into and on to the avocado halves. Sprinkle with parsley and serve.

INGREDIENTS/TO SERVE 6

¼ cup pure olive oil

¼ white wine vinegar

3 tablespoons chopped green onion

¼ teaspoon dried oregano

¼ teaspoon Tabasco sauce

2 cups cooked shrimp

2 large tomatoes, seeded and diced

1 cucumber, peeled and diced

3 tablespoons coarsely chopped pimento-stuffed green olives

½ teaspoon salt

3 tablespoons chopped pimento

½ teaspoon black pepper

3 medium-sized avocados

1 tablespoon fresh lemon juice

6 lettuce leaves

3 tablespoons chopped fresh parsley

● *Photograph opposite, below*

Ham and Vegetable Pasta Salad

INGREDIENTS/TO SERVE 6

1 lb pasta shapes, cooked

2 tablespoons pure olive oil

1 cup uncooked peas

1 cup raw carrots, sliced

1 cup raw broccoli florets

1 cup cooked ham, cubed

¼ cup grated Parmesan cheese

2 tablespoons chopped fresh parsley

1¼ cups Italian Dressing (see page 40)

1 teaspoon freshly ground black pepper

● Photograph opposite

An excellent summer-time main course, and a good way to use leftover ham. Serve this salad with a German Rhine or Mosel white wine.

1. Put the cooked pasta in a salad bowl and add the olive oil. Toss to coat well.
2. Cook the peas, carrots and broccoli in a large pan of boiling water until just tender, about 8 to 10 minutes. Drain and rinse with cold water for 1 minute. Drain well again.
3. Add the vegetables and ham to the pasta. Lightly toss. Add the Parmesan cheese and parsley and toss. Add the Italian dressing and toss well. Sprinkle over the pepper. Chill the salad for 1 hour before serving.

Tortellini Salad

INGREDIENTS/TO SERVE 4

1 lb tortellini, fresh or frozen

½ medium-sized red onion, finely chopped

1 sweet red pepper, seeded and finely chopped

½ cup fresh parsley or basil, chopped

½ cup Creamy Dressing (see page 38)

Tortellini are small, knot-shaped pasta filled with a meat or cheese mixture. Frozen tortellini aren't quite as good as fresh, but they will still do nicely in this recipe. For a meaty variation, add four slices of coarsely chopped prosciutto to the salad.

1. Cook the tortellini in a large pot of salted boiling water until tender, about 6 to 8 minutes. Drain and rinse with cold water. Drain well again.
2. Put the tortellini, onion and red pepper in a salad bowl and toss gently. Add the parsley or basil and the dressing and toss again.

Clam and Pasta Salad

INGREDIENTS/TO SERVE 4-6

½ lb pasta shapes, cooked

½ cup pure olive oil

½ lb cooked clams or mussels, chopped

3 tablespoons fresh lemon juice

1½ garlic cloves, finely chopped

3 tablespoons chopped fresh parsley

2 tablespoons chopped fresh basil

1 tablespoon chopped fresh mint

3 tablespoons freshly grated Parmesan cheese

1 teaspoon salt

1 teaspoon freshly ground black pepper

GARNISH

Lemon Bow garnish (see page 23)

● Photograph opposite

Although it looks like a plate of hot pasta with white clam sauce, this salad is really a cool and refreshing summer variation which is very quick to make. Mussels may be substituted. Serve the salad as a light lunch or as a first course before Italian meat dishes.

1. In a large salad bowl, put the pasta and 1 tablespoon of the olive oil. Lightly toss. Add the clams and toss again.
2. Put the remaining olive oil, lemon juice and garlic in a jar with a tightly fitting lid. Cover tightly and shake until blended. Add the parsley, basil, mint, Parmesan cheese, salt and pepper. Shake again until well mixed. Pour the dressing over the pasta and clams. Toss well.
3. Cover the bowl and chill for 2 hours. Toss well before serving.

Linguini Salad

INGREDIENTS/TO SERVE 4-6

4 large tomatoes, seeded and coarsely chopped

¼ cup marinated artichoke hearts, drained and chopped

4 teaspoons chopped fresh parsley

1 cup Italian Dressing (see page 40)

1 teaspoon Tabasco sauce

1 lb linguini (thin noodles)

This quick and elegant salad is perfect when unexpected guests arrive for lunch. It's also a good accompaniment to veal dishes. Thin spaghetti may be substituted for the linguini.

1. Put the tomatoes, artichoke hearts and parsley in a salad bowl.
2. Put the Italian dressing and Tabasco sauce in a jar with a tightly fitting lid. Cover tightly and shake well.
3. Pour the dressing over the tomatoes and artichoke hearts. Let stand at room temperature for 1 hour.
4. Cook the linguini in a large pan of boiling water until just tender. Drain well and add the linguini to the salad bowl. Toss well and serve.

Italian Rice Salad

INGREDIENTS/TO SERVE 6

1½ cups cooked rice

½ cup cooked ham, cubed

1 tablespoon drained capers

1 large tomato, seeded and chopped

¼ cup freshly grated Parmesan cheese

3 tablespoons pure olive oil

3 tablespoons fresh lemon juice

½ teaspoon salt

½ teaspoon black pepper

1 tablespoon chopped fresh parsley

½ cup marinated artichoke hearts, drained and coarsely chopped

● *Photograph opposite, above*

In Italy, this salad would be made with arborio short-grain rice, but long-grain or even brown rice will work just as well. Italian Rice Salad can be served before or with baked fish, veal or poultry.

1. Put the rice, ham, capers, tomatoes, and Parmesan cheese in a salad bowl. Toss lightly.
2. Put the olive oil, lemon juice, salt, pepper and parsley in a jar with a tightly fitting lid. Cover tightly and shake well.
3. Pour the dressing over the rice salad and toss. Garnish with the artichoke hearts. Let the salad stand at room temperature for 1 hour before serving.

Summer Macaroni Salad

INGREDIENTS/TO SERVE 6-8

¾ cup mayonnaise

2 teaspoons Dijon-style mustard

1 tablespoon white wine vinegar

¼ teaspoon celery seeds

2 cups macaroni, cooked

½ cup celery, chopped

⅓ cup raw carrots, chopped

¼ cup radishes, sliced

3 tablespoons chopped pimento-stuffed green olives

3 tablespoons chopped sweet red pepper

5 tablespoons chopped green onion

2 tablespoons chopped fresh parsley

¾ teaspoon salt

¼ teaspoon freshly ground black pepper

● *Photograph opposite, below*

Contrary to popular belief, macaroni salad is not an excuse to empty the refrigerator of all vegetable leftovers. To avoid a bland, soggy salad, use fresh, not cooked, vegetables and cook the macaroni only until it is tender but still firm. Summer Macaroni Salad goes down extremely well at summer picnics and barbecues.

1. Put the mayonnaise, mustard, vinegar and celery seeds in a small mixing bowl. Beat with a fork or electric beater until well blended.
2. Put the macaroni in a large serving bowl and add the mayonnaise mixture. Toss until the macaroni is well coated. Add the celery, carrots, radishes, olives, red peppers, green onions and parsley. Toss well. Add the salt and pepper. Toss lightly.
3. Cover the bowl and chill for 1½ hours. Remove the salad from the refrigerator and serve.

Tabouleh

Tabouleh is made from burghul wheat, nuggets of wholewheat that have been steamed and broken up. If they were ground instead, the result would be wholewheat flour. Tabouleh is a Lebanese dish served at picnics throughout the Middle East. The fresh mint is a crucial element. It can be increased to taste, but do not decrease it — and never use dried mint. Roast meats go well with tabouleh.

1. Put the burghul in a bowl and add the boiling water. Stir, cover the bowl, and let stand for 35 minutes.
2. Drain the burghul, squeezing out any remaining water between the palms of your hands. Put the burghul in a bowl. Add the green onions, mint, tomatoes and parsley. Toss gently.
3. Add the olive oil. Stir until well mixed. Add the lemon juice, salt and pepper. Stir until well mixed.
4. Serve the tabouleh on a bed of lettuce leaves, garnished with black olives.

INGREDIENTS/TO SERVE 6

1 cup burghul wheat

2 cups boiling water

½ cup green onions, chopped

5 tablespoons chopped fresh mint

2 medium-sized tomatoes, seeded and chopped

1 cup fresh parsley, chopped

5 tablespoons pure olive oil

6 tablespoons fresh lemon juice

½ teaspoon salt

½ teaspoon freshly ground black pepper

10 large lettuce leaves

10 black olives

● Photograph opposite

Chicken and Pasta Salad

This colorful main course salad offers a variety of contrasting textures and tastes.

1. Cook the pasta in boiling, salted water, to which you have added a few drops of oil until *al dente*. Drain and allow to cool.
2. Core the apple but do not peel it, as the rosy color adds interest to the salad. Slice and sprinkle with lemon juice.
3. Toss the salad ingredients together and dress with the mayonnaise, into which you have blended a little turmeric.

INGREDIENTS/TO SERVE 4

1 cup pasta shells

1 rosy-skinned dessert apple

lemon juice

½ cup cooked chicken, diced

6 asparagus spears, cooked and cut into pieces or 1 can asparagus

2 or 3 sticks celery, chopped

½ cup mayonnaise

turmeric to taste

Curried Apricot and Chicken Salad

INGREDIENTS/SERVES 4-6

4 chicken breasts, skinned and boned

4 tablespoons unsalted butter

1 cup unflavored yogurt

¼ cup curry powder

1 teaspoon salt

Freshly ground black pepper to taste

½ lb seedless green grapes

2 cups dried apricots, cut in strips

2 cups mandarin orange segments (if canned, drained)

1 cup cashews

1 cup apricot liqueur

6-8 lettuce leaves

● Photograph opposite, above

A chilled dry white wine is a good accompaniment to this main-course salad. For a spicier flavor add 1 tablespoon of ground cardamom and a pinch of cayenne pepper.

1. Cut the chicken breasts into 1 in (2.5 cm) cubes. Melt the butter in a large skillet. Add the chicken and cook over moderate to low heat, turning often, until the cubes are firm but not brown, about 7 to 10 minutes. Using a slotted spoon, transfer the chicken to a large mixing bowl.

2. In a small bowl, combine the yogurt and curry powder. Mix well. Add the curry mixture to the chicken. Season with salt and pepper and more curry, if desired.

4. Add the grapes, apricots, mandarin orange segments, cashews and apricot liqueur to the chicken. Toss until all the ingredients are well coated. Cover the bowl and refrigerate for at least 1 hour.

4. Line a serving dish with the lettuce leaves. Mound the salad on the lettuce and serve. Garnish with additional fruit and cashews if desired.

Chinese Pork Salad

INGREDIENTS/SERVES 4 TO 6

2 cups fresh mung bean sprouts or alfalfa sprouts

1 medium carrot, peeled and shredded

2 cups roast pork, shredded

2 tablespoons smooth peanut butter

3 tablespoons warm water

½ teaspoon salt

1 tablespoon sugar

1 teaspoon honey

1 tablespoon (30 ml) sesame seed oil

1½ tablespoons white wine vinegar

1 tablespoon peanut oil

1 teaspoon Tabasco sauce

2 garlic cloves, finely chopped

3 tablespoons chopped green onion

GARNISH

Tomato Rose garnish (see page 24)

● Photograph opposite, below

Without using authentic Chinese implements or cooking techniques, this salad still achieves an authentic Chinese flavor. The dressing is good on green salads as well. Serve as an hors-d'oeuvre.

1. Blanch the bean sprouts and carrots in separate pans of boiling water for 10 seconds. Drain and rinse in cold water. Drain well again and pat dry with paper towels.

2. Line a serving plate with the bean sprouts and carrots. Make a mound of the roast pork on top of the bean sprouts and carrots.

3. In a jar with a screw-top lid, combine the peanut butter and warm water. Stir well. Add the salt, sugar, honey, vinegar, sesame seed oil, peanut oil and Tabasco sauce. Cover tightly and shake until well blended. Add the garlic and green onion. Shake again. Pour the dressing over the pork and serve.

Spanish Chicken Salad

INGREDIENTS/TO SERVE 6-8

3 cups cooked chicken, shredded

½ cup salami, cubed

3 medium-sized potatoes, peeled, boiled and diced

1 sweet red or green pepper, seeded and coarsely chopped

½ cup pimento, chopped

1 cup cooked green peas

2 radishes, thinly sliced

2 tablespoons drained capers

½ cup pimento-stuffed green olives, quartered

3 tablespoons dry sherry

½ cup pure olive oil

¼ cup red wine vinegar

¼ teaspoon ground white pepper

1 large head Boston lettuce

2 hard-cooked eggs, chopped

6 to 8 cooked asparagus spears

8 fresh parsley sprigs

1 medium-sized onion, sliced into rings

● Photograph opposite

Leftover chicken returns to the table as a complete, informal meal in this salad. This is a flexible recipe. Feel free to add other crisply cooked or raw vegetables.

1. Put the chicken, salami, potato, chopped pepper, pimento, green peas, radishes, capers and olives in a mixing bowl.
2. Put the sherry, olive oil, vinegar and white pepper in a jar with a tightly fitting lid. Cover tightly and shake until well mixed.
3. Pour the dressing over the salad. Toss well. Cover the bowl and chill for 4 to 6 hours.
4. Line a serving platter with the lettuce leaves.
5. Add the chopped eggs to the salad in the mixing bowl and toss lightly. Drain any excess dressing from the mixing bowl. Transfer the salad from the mixing bowl to the salad dish. Garnish with the asparagus spears, parsley sprigs and onion rings. Serve.

Ham Salad

INGREDIENTS/TO SERVE 6

2 cups ham, diced

1 cup apples, peeled, cored and diced

1 cup celery, diced

½ cup cooked asparagus, coarsely chopped

2 hard-cooked eggs, chopped

2 tablespoons chopped fresh parsley

1 cup Mustard Vinaigrette (see page 35)

½ bunch arugula (optional)

The vinaigrette dressing on this salad makes a change from the traditional mayonnaise. Ham Salad is a good way to use up leftover ham. For a less fruity taste use diced boiled potatoes instead of the apples. When served with your favorite wine (red or white), this salad makes a fine summer meal.

1. Put the ham, apple, celery, asparagus, eggs and parsley in a salad bowl. Toss well.
2. Pour the dressing over the salad and toss lightly. Garnish with the arugula leaves and serve.

Veal Salad with Walnut Dressing

Serve this hearty salad as a main course at lunch or supper along with a good red wine. The veal can be cooked up to two days in advance, but the dressing should be made just before use.

1. Into a large pan, put the veal, carrots, celery, onions, parsley, garlic, black peppercorns and ½ teaspoon of salt. Add enough water to cover. Simmer, covered, over medium to low heat until the veal is tender, about 2 to 2½ hours.
2. When the veal is done, remove it from the pan. (Use the liquid and vegetables remaining in the pan for stock or discard.) When the veal is cool enough to handle, pull the meat apart into pieces that are about ½ × 2 in (1 × 5 cm) in size.
3. Put the veal pieces in a large mixing bowl and add ½ teaspoon of the salt and 2 tablespoons of the walnut oil. Toss.
4. In a small skillet, heat 1 tablespoon of the walnut oil. Add the walnuts and cook, stirring constantly, until browned, about 4 minutes. Remove from the heat and set aside.
5. In a small mixing bowl, combine the remaining walnut oil, vinegar, green peppercorns and remaining salt. Whisk together.
6. Peel the avocados. Cut them in half and remove the stones. Cut each half into 6 long slices. Add the avocado slices to the dressing and toss.
7. Arrange the veal in the center of a serving platter. Arrange the avocado slices around the veal. Top the avocado slices with the browned walnuts. Spoon the dressing over the salad and serve.

INGREDIENTS/TO SERVE 4

3 lb boneless veal shoulder
2 carrots, cut into 2-in/5-cm pieces
2 celery stalks, cut into 2-in/5-cm pieces
3 onions, quartered
8 parsley sprigs
4 garlic cloves
10 whole black peppercorns
1¼ teaspoons salt
½ cup walnut oil
⅓ cup coarsely chopped walnuts
2 tablespoons white wine vinegar
1 teaspoon drained, finely chopped green peppercorns
2 ripe avocados

Italian Mixed Meats Salad

The list of Italian smoked and cured meats is impressive. Usually served as antipasto, not as main-course meats, many of them, including salami and sausages, are made by peasants in the mountain villages, using recipes that have remained unchanged for centuries. Here is a small selection of Italian meats. Arranged decoratively on a large serving platter, these meats make an attractive appetizer.

INGREDIENTS/TO SERVE 4 (from top to bottom)

Prosciutto crudo — a delicate-tasting ham
Salami Ungherese — spicy fat pork
Manzo salato (salt beef)
Pastrami — cured, smoked beef
Salsiccia di Fegato (liver sausage)
Milano Salami — seasoned with garlic, pepper and white wine
Bologna — a mixture of cooked smoked pork and beef

German Beef Salad

When served with a lightly cooked, fresh green vegetable or a side salad of lettuce, cucumber, tomato and onion, this salad makes a substantial main course. If stored in a tightly covered container in the refrigerator, it can be made one to two days in advance.

1. Put the mustard, beef stock, vegetable oil, vinegar, salt and pepper in a jar with a tightly fitting lid. Cover tightly and shake until well mixed.
2. Put the beef, tomatoes, eggs, potatoes, onions and gherkins in a salad bowl. Toss.
3. Pour the dressing over the salad and toss again. Cover the bowl and chill for 1½ hours. Toss lightly and garnish with parsley before serving.

INGREDIENTS/TO SERVE 6

2 tablespoons Dijon mustard

½ cup beef stock

5 tablespoons vegetable oil

¼ cup red wine vinegar

½ teaspoon salt

½ teaspoon freshly ground black pepper

2 lb cooked beef, cubed

2 large tomatoes, diced

2 hard-cooked eggs, chopped

2 large potatoes, peeled, boiled and diced

2 small onions, finely chopped

10 small sweet gherkins, finely chopped

½ cup chopped fresh parsley

GARNISH

Gherkin Fan garnish (see page 24)

● Photograph opposite

Mustard Chicken Salad

The plain mayonnaise in this recipe may be replaced by Curry Mayonnaise I (see page 38) or Curry Mayonnaise II (see page 38). Serve the salad as a main course with a full-bodied, dry red wine.

1. Put the shredded chicken in a mixing bowl.
2. Cut the artichoke hearts into eighths and add them to the chicken. Add the green onions, dill, salt and pepper. Toss lightly.
3. In a bowl mix the mustard with the mayonnaise until smooth. Add the mustard mayonnaise to the chicken salad. Toss well. Cover the bowl and refrigerate for 2 hours.
4. Line a salad bowl with the arugula leaves. Spoon the salad into a mound on top of the arugula and garnish with tomatoes and parsley. Serve.

INGREDIENTS/TO SERVE 6

2 lb cooked chicken breasts, shredded

1 cup cooked artichoke hearts

¼ cup green onions, chopped

3 tablespoons coarsely chopped fresh dill

½ teaspoon salt

½ teaspoon freshly ground black pepper

3 tablespoons Dijon-style mustard

1⅓ cups mayonnaise

1 head arugula

2 large tomatoes, cut into wedges

6 fresh parsley sprigs

Duck Salad

INGREDIENTS/TO SERVE 6–8

3 lb cooked duck, sliced

½ cup shallots, sliced into rings

2 tablespoons white wine vinegar

2 tablespoons fresh orange juice

1 teaspoon Dijon-style mustard

¼ teaspoon salt

3 tablespoons walnut oil

3 tablespoons pure olive oil

1 bunch watercress

½ lb fresh cherries

● Photograph opposite

Duck Salad is best served as one of several choices at a buffet. A bottle of German Rhine wine should be on the buffet table as well to accompany the salad.

1. Put the duck on a serving platter. Add the shallots.
2. Put the vinegar, orange juice, mustard and salt in a small mixing bowl. Stir with a fork until the salt dissolves. Stirring continuously, slowly add the walnut oil and olive oil.
3. Pour the dressing over the duck salad. Add the watercress and cherries and serve.

Ham and Sesame Potato Salad

INGREDIENTS/TO SERVE 4

2 lb potatoes, parboiled and cut into manageable pieces

2 tablespoons sesame seeds

½ lb carrots, grated

¼ cup plump sultanas

¾ cooked ham, diced

1 teaspoon lime juice

oil (sesame seed for choice)

salt and freshly ground pepper

The sesame seeds add an exotic flavor to this rather unusual main course salad.

1. Fry the potatoes in oil and add sesame seeds. Stir until the seeds have coated the potatoes. Transfer to a plate and allow to cool.
2. Toss all ingredients together.
3. Make a dressing of lime juice and sesame oil in a proportion of two to one and pour over the salad.
4. Season with salt and pepper and toss again.

California Waldorf Salad

This recent variation on the Waldorf Salad uses grapes and the ubiquitous bean sprout. Because it is sweeter than the traditional recipe, California Waldorf Salad should be served as a last course or dessert.

1. Blanch the bean sprouts in a pan of boiling water for 45 seconds. Drain and rinse in cold water. Drain well again. Coarsely chop the bean sprouts.
2. Put the apple, celery, almonds and mushrooms in a large mixing bowl. Mix well with a wooden spoon.
3. Add the Yogurt Mayonnaise and mix thoroughly.
4. Line a serving platter with the lettuce leaves. Mound the bean sprouts in the center. Transfer the mixed ingredients to the platter and serve, garnished with the halved grapes.

INGREDIENTS/TO SERVE 6

½ cup mung bean sprouts or alfalfa sprouts

3 tart apples, cored and diced but not peeled

2 cups celery, chopped

¼ cup slivered almonds

3 large mushrooms, coarsely chopped

1 cup Yogurt Mayonnaise (see page 39)

10 lettuce leaves

½ cup seedless grapes, halved

● Photograph opposite, above

Waldorf Salad

Oscar M. Tschirsky, better known simply as Oscar of the Waldorf, was maître d'hôtel of the famed Waldorf Astoria Hotel in New York City from 1893 to 1943. This first-course salad is his invention. The original salad did not call for walnuts, although they are considered indispensable now.

1. Put the apples, celery, walnuts and raisins in a large mixing bowl. Add the lemon juice, mayonnaise and salt and pepper. Stir until well blended.
2. Arrange the salad on a serving platter, garnished with sprigs of chicory and with slices of apple if desired.

INGREDIENTS/TO SERVE 4-6

3 tart apples, cored and diced but not peeled

2 cups celery, chopped

½ cup walnuts, coarsely chopped

3 tablespoons raisins

3 tablespoons fresh lemon juice

¾ cup mayonnaise

1 teaspoon salt

½ teaspoon freshly ground black pepper

● Photograph opposite, below

South Seas Fruit Salad

In the middle of winter, when the sun is a pale cold circle in the sky, this salad will transport you to warm sunny beaches, brilliant blue skies and the gentle waves of a Pacific island, if only for a minute or two.

1. Arrange the papaya, banana, grapes, pineapple and tangerine segments in serving bowls.
2. Into a blender or food processor, put the peanut oil, sesame oil, lime juice, salt and sugar. Blend until well mixed.
3. Pour the dressing over the salad. Cover the bowls and chill for 1 to 2 hours before serving.

INGREDIENTS/TO SERVE 6-8

2 ripe papayas, peeled, seeded and cubed

2 large bananas, peeled and diced

½ cup seedless green grapes, halved

1 cup pineapple, cubed

3 tangerines, peeled, white membrane removed, segmented and seeded

5 tablespoons peanut oil

1 tablespoon sesame oil

¼ cup fresh lime juice

¼ teaspoon salt

2 tablespoons sugar

● *Photograph opposite*

Strawberry and Avocado Salad

This very attractive salad can be served as a starter, as an accompaniment to plain white meat, fish or egg dishes, or as an unusual dessert.

1. Cut avocado in half lengthwise and remove stone. Carefully remove flesh from shell in one piece, using a metal spoon or pallet knife. Cut each half into slices and arrange around the edge of the serving plate.
2. Hull and slice the strawberries. Pile in the middle of the plate.
3. Mix together the strawberry vinegar and olive oil and pour over salad. Season with lots of black pepper.

INGREDIENTS/TO SERVE 2

1 ripe avocado

½ cup strawberries

1 tablespoon strawberry vinegar

1 tablespoon olive oil

plenty of freshly ground black pepper

Melon Salad with Ginger Sauce

INGREDIENTS/TO SERVE 6-8

¾ cup whipping cream

1 teaspoon fresh lemon juice

1 tablespoon superfine sugar

⅛ teaspoon cayenne pepper

3 large pieces preserved ginger, finely chopped

¼ cup almonds, chopped

1 large honeydew melon, peeled, seeded and cubed

● Photograph opposite, above

A French Sauternes or Spanish sherry makes a pleasant accompaniment to this salad. It's a particularly good way to end a dinner consisting of poultry.

1. Put the cream, lemon juice, sugar and cayenne pepper in a mixing bowl. Beat or whisk the cream until it becomes thick but not stiff. Add the ginger and the almonds, reserving 1 tablespoon of the almonds. Continue to beat or whisk until the cream becomes stiff. Cover the bowl and chill until ready to serve.
2. Put the melon in a serving dish and chill until ready to serve.
3. Just before serving, top the melon cubes with the ginger cream. Sprinkle the remaining almonds on top and serve.

Pear Salad

INGREDIENTS/TO SERVE 4

4 Bartlett pears

1 clove garlic, crushed

1 teaspoon salt

1½ teaspoons sugar

½ teaspoon dried tarragon, crumbled

½ teaspoon dried basil, crumbled

¼ cup red wine vinegar

¼ cup olive oil

¼ cup water

1 tablespoon sherry

1 cup celery, coarsely chopped

1 cup green pepper, coarsely chopped

½ cup green onions, sliced

2 large ripe tomatoes, finely chopped

4 romaine lettuce leaves, chilled

An unusual juxtaposition of fruit and vegetables, this salad is light and refreshing, ideal as a starter.

1. Wash the pears and refrigerate.
2. In a bowl mix together the garlic, salt, and sugar. Add the tarragon, basil, vinegar, oil, water and sherry. Whisk until well blended. Transfer to a 16-ounce (½ litre) jar, cover, and let stand for 1 to 1½ hours.
3. Place the celery, green pepper, green onions and tomatoes in a bowl. Chill 1 hour.
4. Remove the vegetables and pears from the refrigerator. Shake the dressing to mix well. Pour half the dressing over the vegetables and toss.
5. Place 1 lettuce leaf on each of 4 serving plates.
6. Halve and core the pears. Arrange 2 pear halves, cut-side up, on each lettuce leaf. Top with the dressed vegetables. Spoon the remaining dressing over the pears and serve.

Champagne and Peach Salad

Don't use your best Champagne for this salad. Substitute 3 cups fresh strawberries when they are in season for the peaches. Serve the salad with small cups of rich espresso coffee.

1. Prick the peach slices with a fork.
2. Put the orange juice, lime juice, cinnamon and sugar in a jar with a tightly fitting lid. Cover tightly and shake well.
3. Put the peaches in a serving bowl and add the orange juice mixture. Add the Champagne and toss gently. Cover the bowl and chill the salad for 2 to 3 hours. Serve in small bowls.

INGREDIENTS/TO SERVE 6

6 ripe peaches, peeled, stoned and thinly sliced

3 tablespoons fresh orange juice

1 tablespoon fresh lime juice

⅛ teaspoon cinnamon

1 tablespoon superfine sugar

2 cups Champagne

● *Photograph opposite, above*

Sunshine Fruit Salad

With its touches of orange and red, this salad is a study of the golden hues of the sun. Fruit Salad Syrup Dressing (see page 43) may be substituted for the maple syrup. If you do this, add an additional tablespoon of crème de cacao for extra flavor.

1. Halve the grapefruits. Without piercing the skins, remove the grapefruit segments. Remove as much of the white membrane as possible from the segments, seed them, and break them apart. Reserve the grapefruit-skin shells.
2. Combine the grapefruit segments, banana, mandarin orange segments, pineapple and chopped cherries in a mixing bowl. Toss lightly. Add the maple syrup and crème de cacao. Toss lightly again.
3. Fill the grapefruit shells with the fruit salad. Top each salad with a whole maraschino cherry. Refrigerate until ready to serve.

INGREDIENTS/TO SERVE 4

2 grapefruits

1 cup banana, thinly sliced

½ cup mandarin orange segments (if canned, drained)

1 cup pineapple wedges

1 tablespoon red maraschino cherries, finely chopped

3 tablespoons pure maple syrup

1 tablespoon crème de cacao

4 red maraschino cherries

● *Photograph opposite, below*

Caribbean Fruit Salad

Children love this salad — and so do their parents. Needless to say, all the fruit must be as fresh as possible, but if you cannot obtain fresh blueberries, use frozen ones instead.

1. Arrange the blueberries, peaches, grapes, pineapple, honeydew melon, tangerines, cantaloup melon, cheese and dates on a large platter.
2. In a small mixing bowl, add the honey and rum to the Yogurt Mayonnaise and stir until well mixed. Place the dressing in a separate bowl in the center of the platter.
3. Lightly roll the banana pieces in the chopped almonds and add them to the rest of the fruit. Let each guest take some fruit and dressing and toss the salad on individual plates.

INGREDIENTS/TO SERVE 6–8

1 cup blueberries or blackcurrants

1 cup peaches, stoned and thinly sliced

1 cup green and black seedless grapes, halved

1 cup fresh pineapple chunks

1 cup honeydew melon, sliced

5 tangerines, peeled, white membrane removed, segmented and seeded

1 cup cantaloup melon, sliced

1 cup Gruyère cheese, cubed

1 cup fresh dates

1 cup Yogurt Mayonnaise (see page 39)

1 tablespoon honey

2 tablespoons rum

2 large bananas, halved

½ cup almonds, finely chopped

● Photograph opposite

Persimmon Salad

Persimmons or 'apples of the Orient' are colorful and decorative and make a very unusual salad starter.

1. Place the persimmons stem-side down on a flat surface. Carefully cut an × into the top surface of the skin. Gently peel the skin away from the pulp, a little bit at a time, about halfway down the side of the persimmon. Keeping the skin intact, loosen the remaining pulp from the skin with a spoon. Place each persimmon on a lettuce leaf.
2. In a small bowl combine the yogurt and lemon juice. Spoon equal amounts over each persimmon and sprinkle with the chopped nuts. Serve immediately or chill briefly.

INGREDIENTS/TO SERVE 4

4 very ripe persimmons

4 crisp butter lettuce leaves

4 tablespoons plain yogurt or sour cream

1 teaspoon lemon juice

½ cup chopped raw cashews

Index

The publishers would like to thank the following for the loan of china, glassware and kitchen equipment:

The Reject China Shop, Beauchamp Place, Knightsbridge, London SW1

David Mellor (kitchen supplies), Covent Garden, London WC2

Liberty, Regent Street, London W1

Moulinex Ltd.